Office Procedures

Other titles in this series

Bookkeeping and Accounting
Business Calculations
Business Communication
Business Law
Business Studies
Keyboarding
Secretarial Duties
The Business of Government
Typing
Word Processing

Office Procedures

Ruth Martindale, RSADip, JEBTDipWP, spent several years as a senior secretary/personal assistant before becoming a Lecturer in Secretarial Studies. She has been an RSA Senior Examiner for many years and has written articles on office procedures and text for secretarial examinations. She currently runs her own Word Processing training centre and bureau service.

Office Procedures

Ruth Martindale

Consultant Editor: Joyce Stananought

Chambers *Commerce Series*

© Ruth Martindale 1988

Published by W & R Chambers Ltd Edinburgh, 1988

British Library Cataloguing in Publication Data

Martindale, Ruth
    Office procedures—(Chambers commerce series)
    1. Office practice
    I. Title
    651   HF5547.5
ISBN 0 550 20711-2

Typeset by Blackwood Pillans & Wilson Ltd. Edinburgh and London

Printed in Great Britain by
Richard Clay Ltd, Bungay, Suffolk

Contents

Acknowledgements   ix

Preface   x

Chapter 1   Types of Employer

1.1   Private Enterprise   1
1.2   Public Enterprise   3
1.3   Co-operatives   3
1.4   Franchise   4
      Questions   4

Chapter 2   Internal Organisation

2.1   Departmental Responsibilities   5
2.2   Responsibilities of a Board of Directors   6
2.3   Responsibilities of a Company Secretary   7
2.4   Centralised Services   7
2.5   The Office Environment   7
2.6   Office Design   9
      Questions   9

Chapter 3   Mail Handling

3.1   Mail Handling   10
3.2   Outgoing Mail   12
3.3   Reference Books   17
      Questions   17

Chapter 4   Postal Services

4.1   Royal Mail Inland Services   18
4.2   Royal Mail International Services   24
4.3   Additional Post Office Services   26
4.4   Alternative Express Services   27
      Questions   28

Chapter 5   Telecommunications

5.1	Telephones	29
5.2	Telephone Services	33
5.3	Telecommunication Services	35
5.4	Integration	38
	Questions	39

Chapter 6   Receiving Visitors

6.1	Reception Duties	40
6.2	Security	42
6.3	Personal Qualities	42
6.4	Dealing with the Press	42
6.5	Reception Area	43
	Questions	43

Chapter 7   Written Communication

7.1	House Style	44
7.2	Composition of Letters	44
7.3	Writing a Memorandum	45
7.4	Displaying an Effective Notice	46
7.5	Bulletins	46
7.6	House Journals	46
7.7	Newsletters	46
7.8	Telex Messages	46
7.9	Telemessages	47
7.10	Presenting a Report	47
7.11	Summaries	47
7.12	Invitations and Replies	48
	Questions	50

Chapter 8   Visual Aids

8.1	Line Graphs	51
8.2	Bar Charts	52
8.3	Sector Charts	53
8.4	Pictograms	53
8.5	Z Charts	53
8.6	Break-Even Charts	55
8.7	Gantt Charts	55
8.8	Pie Charts	56
8.9	Flow Charts	58
8.10	Visual Planning/Control Boards	58
	Questions	59

Chapter 9   Meetings

9.1	Types of Business Meeting	60
9.2	Documents	61
9.3	Duties of the Chairman	65
9.4	Duties of the Secretary	65
9.5	Glossary of Terms	65
	Questions	69

Chapter 10   Record Keeping

10.1	Centralised Records	70
10.2	Decentralised Records	70
10.3	Filing Equipment	71
10.4	Card Holders	73
10.5	Classification	76
10.6	Guides	77
10.7	Colour Codes	78
10.8	Cross Reference	78
10.9	Out Cards	78
10.10	Follow-up Systems	78
10.11	Computer Records	79
	Questions	81

Chapter 11   Electronic Equipment

11.1	Typewriters	82
11.2	Dictating Machines	84
11.3	Word Processors	85
11.4	Microwriter	86
11.5	Facsimile (Fax)	87
11.6	Computers	88
11.7	Printers	92
	Questions	93

Chapter 12   Reprography

12.1	Electrostatic Copier	94
12.2	Dyeline (Diazo) Copier	95
12.3	Duplicators	96
12.4	Heat Copier	97
12.5	Dual Spectrum Copier	97
12.6	Colour Transfer	97
12.7	Offset Litho Printer	98
12.8	Electronic Scanner	99
	Questions	99

Chapter 13   Finding the Facts

13.1	Telephone/Personal Calls	100
13.2	Books	100
13.3	Viewdata/Videotex	102
13.4	Databases	103
	Questions	104

Chapter 14   Stock Control

14.1	Types of Stock	105
14.2	Stock Records	105
14.3	Office Supplies	107
14.4	Inventories	108
14.5	Valuation	109
14.6	Computerised Stock Control	109
	Questions	110

Chapter 15   Sales/Purchasing

15.1	Requisition	111
15.2	Letter of Enquiry	111
15.3	Quotation	113
15.4	Order	114
15.5	Advice/Delivery Notes	115
15.6	Goods Received Note	115
15.7	Invoice	115
15.8	Credit/Debit Notes	116
15.9	Statement	116
15.10	Computerised Procedures	117
	Questions	118

Chapter 16   Methods of Payment

16.1	Bank Services	119
16.2	Post Office Services	126
16.3	Building Societies	128
16.4	Electronic Funds Transfer	129
	Questions	129

Chapter 17   Accounts Department

17.1	Computerised Accounting	131
17.2	Accounting Terms	131
17.3	Petty Cash	132
17.4	Salaries and Wages	135
17.5	Cash Analysis	139
17.6	Computerised Payroll	141
	Questions	141

Index   143

Acknowledgements

The author wishes to thank the following for their assistance:

British Railways Board
British Telecom
H M Stationery Office
National Girobank plc
TSI Publications Ltd
The Post Office (Design Division)
Trainlines of Britain

Preface

This book should prove valuable to all college students and school pupils who are following business or office studies courses, full or part-time. It includes the main topics covered in the syllabuses for all Office Practice, Office Procedures and Secretarial Duties examinations set by the major boards—RSA, Pitman, LCCI, Scotvec and BTEC. It is also an appropriate text where these subjects form a part of a group certificate. It is intended as a textbook but should also serve as an excellent revision text to back up work done from other sources.

It is written in a straightforward concise style, concentrating on the important points and avoiding lengthy detailed descriptions. Whilst explaining the traditional procedures and practices, considerable attention is paid to the modern computerised techniques now used in many offices.

The book is divided into chapters, each of which is divided into numbered sections for easy reference. Each section deals with a different aspect of the main topic. Clear illustrations are included throughout the book. At the end of each chapter there are *Test Yourself* questions designed to assess learning.

R.M.

Chapter 1

Types of Employer

In the UK we have a 'mixed economy', i.e. there are both privately and publicly owned organisations of all sizes providing the services and producing the goods we require.

1.1 Private Enterprise

Sole trader

A person enters business on his/her own, selecting premises and providing (or borrowing) capital. This individual makes all the decisions and reaps the profits or bears all losses. Capital may be limited, so preventing expansion or updating, and without wide expertise he/she may make bad decisions which affect trade. Personal possessions can be taken to repay debts and business may be lost during absence for illness and holidays.

Partnership

A number of people (usually limited to 20) may form a partnership, whereby they are jointly responsible for providing capital, decision-making and sharing profits or losses. The capital and expertise is generally greater than for a sole trader and individual absence affects business less. The partners are liable for each other's actions and can still lose personal possessions to repay large losses. A Deed of Partnership is drawn up setting out the basis for trading.

Limited partnership

All except one of the partners may have limited liability, whereby they cannot lose more than their investment in the company. Personal possessions cannot be seized but a limited partner cannot be involved in the management of, or work within, the company.

A limited partnership must be registered with the Registrar of Companies.

Limited companies (joint stock companies)

These organisations, registered with the Registrar of Companies, have their own identity and may be private (Ltd) or public (PLC) companies. The owners are shareholders with their liability for debts limited to their investment.

They are controlled by a Board of Directors elected by the shareholders, to whom they report annually. Some directors are working executives, e.g. Managing Director, Company Secretary.

Private companies can keep ownership and control closer by restricting the shareholders to family members or known persons. The shares of public companies are offered on the Stock Exchange and can be purchased by anyone. This can lead to a company having a large number of shareholders, when ownership and control of the company become separated. Public limited companies must register two documents:

Memorandum of Association
stating:

       name of company and full address
       liability of members
       share capital details
       objects clauses
       details of subscribers (minimum 7)

Articles of Association
governing the relationship between the company and its members and including:

       how share capital alterations must be made
       rules regarding meetings
       rules governing directors' activities/responsibilities.

Holding companies

An organisation which owns 51% or more of the voting shares of another is known as a holding (or parent) company with the 'owned' company as a subsidiary. Companies with foreign holdings are called multinationals.

1.2 Public Enterprise

Public corporations

Some large organisations, especially service industries, are 'publicly owned', i.e. they are financed and controlled by the State on behalf of the people. They include British Rail, British Coal and the Bank of England. They are set up by Royal Charter or Act of Parliament and directed by a government minister, who appoints the members of the Management Board. Many public corporations have recently been 'privatised'—changed into plcs by the sale of shares—e.g. British Telecom and British Gas.

Consumer Councils exist to protect the interests of the public in the running of these corporations, but council members are appointed by the minister and the councils generally lack sufficient finance to operate effectively.

Central government departments

The Government controls the work of many centralised departments, i.e. Health and Social Security, Education and Science, Defence, the Environment, etc. A minister is appointed to head each department, sometimes with assistants, and the permanent employees are civil servants. The ministers of the major departments are members of the government Cabinet.

Local (municipal) government

Many services and facilities are organised on a local basis, and local councils are responsible for them, i.e. refuse collection, sports facilities, schools, etc. Each section has a permanent staff of officers, but the local councillors, who decide the policies, are elected by the residents. Decisions are made by committees of councillors and usually reflect their political strength.

1.3 Co-operatives

A co-operative is an enterprise jointly owned by its members— employees, friends, relations or suppliers. There is an appointed or elected management team to make decisions on day-to-day business. All members may have limited liability if it is not registered as a limited liability company.

Wholesale/retail

The members (shareholders) of a co-operative are the consumers who share the profits and elect the Management Committee. The co-operative benefits from bulk-buying which individual traders could not afford. The Co-operative Wholesale and Retail Societies have suffered from lack of investment in expansion and updating until recently and they experience keen competition from supermarkets. Groups of farmers are organised into co-operatives for efficient marketing of their produce. In some areas of the country other services are available. There is the Co-operative Bank.

Worker

Industrial co-operatives have multiplied in recent years as workers have invested savings, often redundancy payments, to take over the company in which they work. In the UK many have proved unsuccessful due to limited capital and lack of management expertise. Some receive direct or indirect government finance. The Industrial Common Ownership Act 1976 and the National Co-operative Development Agency regulate their formation and activities. Many subscribe to the non-profit-making ethos.

1.4   Franchise

This is a rapidly growing form of business where an existing brand or product name is 'bought' to start up or expand a business. The franchisor sets out the rules of trading such as style of presentation, stationery, prices, recipes. The franchisee (person operating the new or enlarged business) pays a fee for help and advice, and royalties or commission on sales. Examples include Wimpy, Prontaprint.

Questions

1   What are the disadvantages of being a sole trader?
2   What benefits are there to a director of a joint stock company compared with a partner?
3   Which services are provided by your local government?
4   What is a co-operative? Can you name any co-operative business in your area?

Chapter 2

Internal Organisation

Owners of small companies can directly control and organise their businesses and be closely involved in all aspects of the work. When a company is larger, or expands, and some control is delegated to managers, it is essential that good internal communication and co-ordination exist. Efficient procedures must be initiated and the workforce organised to guide this process. The work is generally divided by type into departments, under the control of managers (grouped into divisions in very large organisations). Each department consists of a number of sections controlled by junior managers or supervisors.

2.1 Departmental Responsibilities

It is common for companies to produce a chart to show this organisation, but each company is unique and the division of responsibilities varies widely.

Fig. 2.1 A typical organisation chart

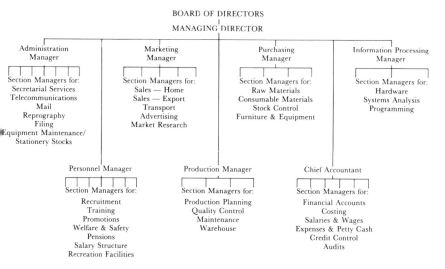

5

Other possible departments may be: export, advertising, research. Outside agencies may be employed for some purposes, e.g. recruitment, printing, data processing or organisation and methods.

Fig. 2.2   Departmental chart

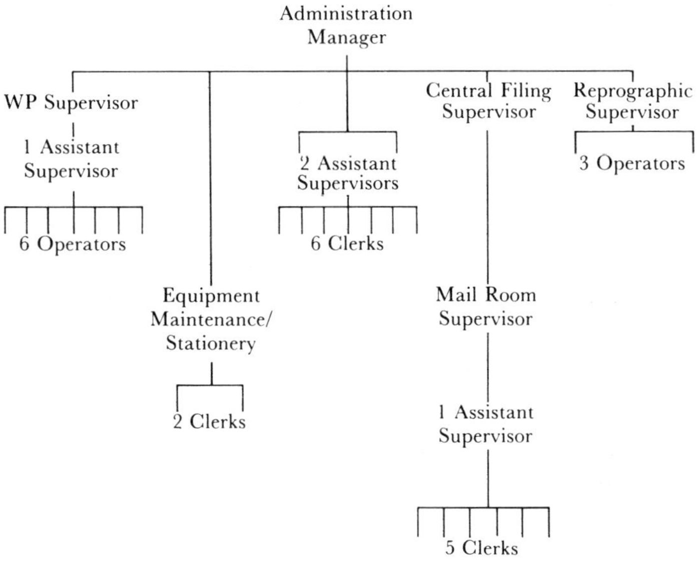

Administration
Manager

WP Supervisor

1 Assistant
Supervisor

6 Operators

2 Assistant
Supervisors

6 Clerks

Central Filing
Supervisor

Reprographic
Supervisor

3 Operators

Equipment
Maintenance/
Stationery

2 Clerks

Mail Room
Supervisor

1 Assistant
Supervisor

5 Clerks

2.2   Responsibilities of a Board of Directors

Management has a responsibility to shareholders, employees and the general public. They should:

— ensure compliance with company law;
— determine policy; clarify objectives and plans;
— ensure sources of capital, initially and continuously;
— establish proper organisation; appoint executives;
— consider company results and report to shareholders;
— ensure good morale, effective leadership and communication;
— earn maximum profits;
— pay dividends to shareholders from profits;
— produce the required quantity of goods of merchantable quality;
— maintain a good relationship with the community;
— maintain a good working relationship with employees.

2.3 Responsibilities of a Company Secretary

A company secretary usually has a legal or financial background and his duties reflect his expertise. Generally the main responsibilities are:

— convening directors' and shareholders' meetings;
— preparing legal documents and contracts;
— ensuring company complies with legal requirements, i.e. registration, provision of data to the Registrar, etc.;
— handling share transactions and maintaining register of shareholders;
— preparing statutory documents and issuing policy statements;
— investing pension funds;
— approving executive and senior appointments;
— fulfilling other duties dependent on company organisation.

2.4 Centralised Services

Sections which provide a service to the whole company may be 'centralised', that is they are organised as one larger unit rather than split into small units within separate departments. These may include filing, typing, reprography, mail room and information processing.

The arrangement gives more effective control, better supervision, better utilisation of equipment and evens out fluctuations in workload between sections and individuals. It usually requires less equipment and fewer employees, whose expertise is greater in their particular occupation. However, increased bureaucracy and delays often result and employees may complain of boredom due to the lack of variety in their work, reduced job satisfaction and motivation.

2.5 The Office Environment

The office or administrative function within an organisation is mostly as a servicing and co-ordinating unit. The main functions include: receiving, recording, distributing and storing information; the arrangement and presentation of information to management. It is the centre of the company's communications and is responsible for the control and protection of the enterprise by inspection, checking, auditing and safeguarding cash and assets. 'The Office' often consists of small units within departments which specialise in their respective duties. Offices may be designed on an open plan or cellular layout.

Fig. 2.3   Office Plans

(a) Open plan

(b) Cellular plan

Open plan

In this layout all sections are in one large area, which is often divided by low partitions and may be 'landscaped'. This puts a greater emphasis on decor and design with colour co-ordination, artwork, plants, etc. to soften the environment. The design is usually handled by a specialist firm.

Advantages	*Disadvantages*
cheaper construction	impersonal
easier maintenance and cleaning	lacks privacy
	more noise and distraction
easier supervisory control	not suitable for noisy machinery
easy communication	
better use of equipment; often less equipment needed	heating/ventilation levels do not suit everybody

Advantages	*Disadvantages*
cheaper heating, lighting, decorating	more rapid spread of illness
less space needed	disputes *re* status
layout follows work flow	
design easily changed	

Cellular

This is the traditional layout of 'closed' individual offices for managers and small units, which is still popular. Employees often prefer this layout particularly for work needing a high level of concentration and for privacy. It also ensures that noisy equipment does not disturb other sections. This layout is more expensive to build, heat and maintain. It also requires a greater floor area.

2.6   Office Design

The space available should be planned carefully considering the type of work, furniture and equipment involved. It is also essential to comply with the Health and Safety at Work Act and Offices, Shops and Railway Premises Act.

Good design would:

— conform to legislation on space, heat, light, etc.;
— consider work flow to minimise movement and accidents;
— provide 'functional areas', grouping similar work;
— use standardised equipment;
— allow privacy and confidentiality;
— be flexible and maximise floor space;
— minimise cost and maintenance;
— ensure ease of supervision and communication;
— consider visual effects: use of colour, texture, fabrics for ideal working conditions;
— consider ergonomics: posture-designed furniture, acoustic covers for equipment, anti-glare screens, etc.

Questions

1   What are the main departments in a manufacturing business?
2   List the responsibilities of the Personnel Department.
3   Which services in a company may be centralised and what advantages are gained by the company with this arrangement?
4   List the advantages of open plan office layout.

Chapter 3

Mail Handling

3.1 Incoming mail

All organisations need an efficient routine for handling their mail. In a small company dealing with mail may be just a part of one person's duties. A large organisation may employ many people in a centralised mail section. The procedure used in a large organisation is easily adapted to a smaller company.

Fig. 3.1 Incoming mail

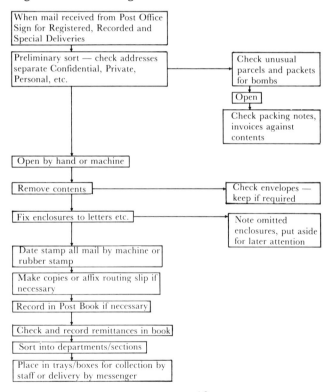

Date stamping

This is done by rubber stamp for small quantities. For larger amounts machines may be electric and may also include the time and other company information.

Letter opener

These machines may be manual or electric. A cut of $\frac{1}{16}"$ is made from the top of the envelope, so ensure that the contents are clear of this area.

Fig. 3.2   Electric letter opener

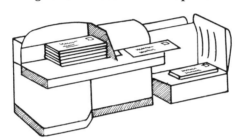

Remittance book

When payments are received through the post, details should be recorded in the remittance book.

Fig. 3.3   Example of remittance book

Date	Customer's Name	Method of Payment	Account No.	Amount £	p	Signature
25/1/88	Carpenter Bros	Cheque	19123	120	50	
''	J Gardner	''	19117	46	78	J Smith
	Barnes & Co	''	18765	95	43	

Routing/circulation slip

When catalogues, reports or journals are received and several members of staff need to see them, it is usual to attach a circulation list. The employees then pass the item on when they have seen it.

Fig. 3.4   A circulation list

CIRCULATION LIST Please read and pass on quickly.		
	Initials	Date
R Fisher		
J Stokes		
G Brown		
N Walker		
P Blackwell		
R Hunter-Smith		
Please return to Mr T Willson.		

Copier

If a document needs attention from more than one person, the quickest method of dealing with it is to make a copy for each person so they can respond promptly. Mail room equipment generally includes a small copier for this purpose.

3.2   Outgoing Mail

Figure 3.5 shows a flow chart of this procedure and this applies to any volume of mail. A variety of equipment is available to speed up this process.

Fig. 3.5 Outgoing mail procedure

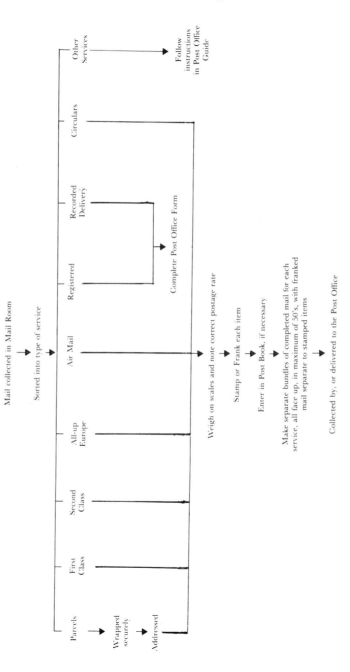

Scales

Accurate scales are essential. Electronic scales, which are widely used, can be programmed with up-to-date postal charges. When an item is weighed the weight and correct postage are displayed.

Fig. 3.6   Electronic scales

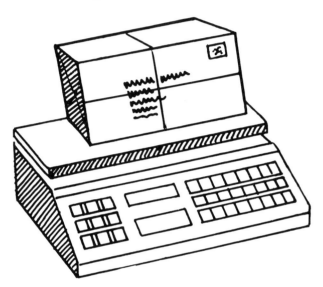

Franking machine

This machine may be electric or electronic. It prints the postage value and date on envelopes or labels. It may also print a slogan or motif. It may have auto-feed and/or a stacking tray. Some machines can be connected to electronic scales: when an item is weighed the correct postage value is set on the franking machine and the envelope or label is printed automatically. Postage units must be purchased in advance. Depending on the type of machine used, this may involve taking the machine to the Post Office for resetting or purchasing plastic cards of credit from the Post Office. The latest electronic models can be reset via the telephone and computer link (Remote Meter Resetting System), with the value invoiced to the company.

Fig. 3.7 A franking machine

The franking machine provides several advantages.

— *Speed.* Several thousand items can be handled each hour.
— *Security.* It is lockable to prevent unauthorised use. It also eliminates the need for large stocks of valuable stamps.
— *Convenience.* It eliminates the need for a Post Book.
— *Accounting control.* It provides an accurate record of expenditure.
— *Advertising.* It saves the cost of printing on envelopes.
— *Despatch.* Mail receives quicker Post Office handling.

There are some disadvantages too.

— Incorrect value may be franked. (If the envelopes and labels are presented to the Post Office a refund is given.)
— It is not economic for small quantities due to the rental or purchase costs.
— Without a Post Book there is no record of addressees for later reference.
— A small stock of stamps may be necessary for late mail, and if credit runs out or the machine breaks down.

It is necessary to have a licence from the Post Office and to complete a Control Card (Fig. 3.8) giving details of daily and weekly use.

Fig. 3.8   Franking machine control card

FRANKING MACHINE CONTROL CARD			PLEASE CHECK DATE DAILY

FRANKING MACHINE CONTROL CARD
User . . . .
Machine   Setting or
(or Meter) No . . . . Recording Unit . . . .
Setting Office
(as shown on Record Card) . . . .
            I certify that the following entries for the above machine for the week
ended . . . . are correct
and that the correct date has been shown on each day's posting.

PLEASE
CHECK
DATE
DAILY

Initial the column below to show date has been changed		ALL MACHINES Reading of Ascending Register (Totalisator)	LOCKING MACHINES Reading of Descending Register (Credit Meter)	ALL MACHINES Last entry in col. "Total Deposits" or "Total Settings" on Record Card
	Mon.			
	Tue.			
	Wed.			
	Thur.			
	Fri.			
	Sat.			

NOTE 1.   This card should be posted on Saturday (or on Friday if no postings are made on Saturday) whether or not the machine has been used in that week.   Signed . . . .

. . . . .19. . . . . .

NOTE 2.   The daily entry must be made on completion of each day's postings.   Post Office Examining Officer's initials . . . .

Addressing machines

When a company sends mail to the same addresses repeatedly, they may use prepared masters on an addressing machine to speed up the procedure of printing on labels, envelopes or documents (to be used with window envelopes). Masters can be on stencil or spirit plates (for occasional use or limited life) or embossed in foil, plastic or metal plates (for frequent or long-term use). The larger machines can be programmed to skip or repeat plates.

Many companies now computerise their mailing list and print it on self-adhesive labels, and equipment is available to stick these on to envelopes.

Computerised mail room equipment

A company which sends a large quantity of circulars or similar documents, would deal with their requirements rapidly and reduce staff or release them for other work by using electronic equipment. Computerised mailing systems are available which separate sheets, fold, insert, seal and frank. They may be linked to label printers and incorporate fixing the labels to the envelopes.

Additional equipment

There are machines to handle separate functions and speed up the preparation of outgoing mail.

Folding machine

This may be manual or electric and gives up to three folds (adjustable) per A4 sheet. It may have auto-feed.

Sealing machine

This is electric and may have auto-feed; it can handle large quantities of self-sealing or gummed envelopes.

Inserting and sealing machine

This electric machine collates up to eight pages, opens the envelope flap, inserts papers, moistens flap, seals, franks, counts and stacks items. It will handle photographs, wallpaper samples, capsules, etc. at speeds up to 6000 items per hour.

3.3   Reference Books

The Post Office Guide, which is published annually with regular supplements, includes all current information on mail handling.

Questions

1   List the equipment you can use when handling incoming mail.
2   What would you do if an enclosure was mentioned but not received?
3   What types of mail would you not open?
4   State the types of mail for which the Post Office requires a signature on delivery.
5   List the advantages of using a franking machine.
6⁻ Explain what you would do if a clerk incorrectly franked several items of today's post.
7   Your company sends several thousand circulars to a regular mailing list of customers twice a month. Write a memo to the Office Manager listing specific equipment to aid this work.

Chapter 4

Postal Services

A wide choice of services is available to business for the delivery of mail. Mostly these are provided by the Post Office, but there are other suppliers of some services.

The Post Office has four main sections: two deal with mail services, two with counter services and the National Girobank. For all special Post Office services a form must be completed, then the items handed over the counter, or bundled separately if collected from company premises. Discounts are available to bulk users of many services. The main services to business are given in this chapter.

4.1 Royal Mail Inland Services

Letters and packets

First Class post
This would be used for much of a company's mail. Next day delivery is not guaranteed but latest posting times are issued for all areas. The cost depends on the weight of individual items.

Second Class post
This is often recommended by companies for non-urgent items as it is cheaper. The cost also depends on weight, and delivery should be within three days.

Business Reply Service
This service allows customers to contact a company without incurring any postal expense. The business must have a licence from the Post Office and will be charged a fee for each item received plus the chosen First or Second Class postal rate. Preprinted stationery must be provided for all Business Reply items (Fig. 4.1).

Fig. 4.1   Business reply service

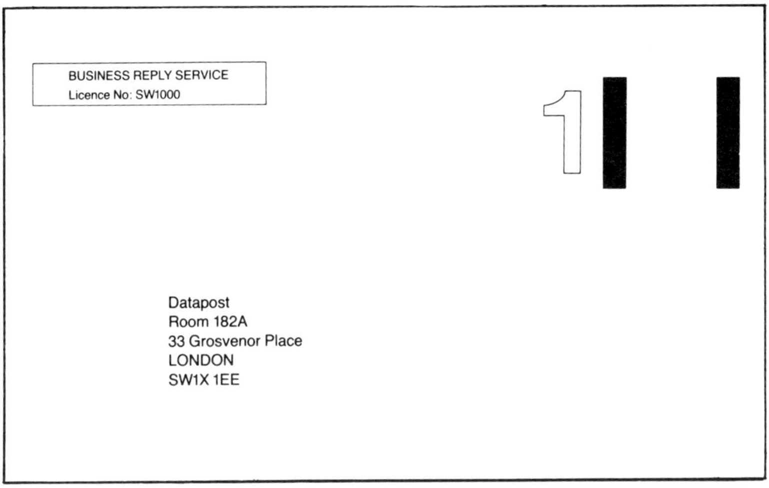

Freepost

This service is designed to encourage potential customers to make enquiries or answer advertisements without incurring any postal expense. When the customer's own stationery is used, i.e. to answer a newspaper advertisement, the word FREEPOST must be included in the address and items will travel Second Class. Preprinted stationery may be provided for First or Second Class replies to direct mail shots and special offers. Discounts are available to large users of these services.

Admail

This is a redirection response service which enables advertisers to quote a local or prestigious address but have the replies redirected to another address in the UK. Discounts are available to companies having more than one Admail contract. This service can be combined with Freepost.

Special Delivery

Next day delivery is guaranteed by the Post Office, the item being delivered by messenger if it arrives too late for inclusion with the first postal delivery of the day. The charge is First Class rate, plus a fee. A certificate of posting (Fig. 4.2) is provided but items must be handed in by the published 'latest recommended posting time'. This service is not available to the Channel Islands, Isle of Man or Irish Republic.

Fig. 4.2   Special delivery form

Express Delivery

A service for letters and packets which is available to the Isle of Man and Channel Islands only and for letters and parcels to the Irish Republic. Items travel by ordinary mail from posting to delivery offices but are then sent by special messenger during certain hours, if this is quicker than normal handling.

Railway Letter

First Class mail may be handed in at the parcels office of a main line station. On receipt at the destination station it may be delivered by Post Office messenger, collected by the addressee or put in a post box for normal delivery.

Datapost

This is a same day or overnight courier service using special bags or envelopes. Customers may have a regular contract or may telephone for use of the service as required. Door-to-door collection and delivery is available and items carry free insurance. There is a minimum charge and exact cost depends on weight.

Fig. 4.3   Datapost marking

Datapost

Registered Post

This service is designed for sending items of value, i.e. cash, jewellery, etc. Use of the special stationery is recommended. The charge includes an insurance fee which is dependent on the value of the goods and compensation is paid for loss in accordance with the scale. A form must be completed at the time of mailing and proof of posting is given. Advice of delivery is available, if requested at the time of posting, as a signature is required on delivery. Registered Post is handled separately from other services and receives extra security.

Fig. 4.4   Registered post label

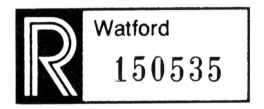

Recorded Delivery

This service is designed for sending items of importance such as documents but not for cash or other valuable items. Compensation is paid for loss to a maximum of £18. A form is completed and proof of posting is received. Advice of delivery is available, if requested at the time of posting, as a signature is always required on delivery. Items are handled with First Class mail, there being no special security.

Fig. 4.5   Recorded delivery form

W	**Recorded Delivery**

Certificate of Posting for Recorded Delivery

How to post

1 Enter below in ink the name and full address as written on the letter or packet.
2 Affix the numbered adhesive label in the top left-hand corner of the letter (or close to the address on a packet).
3 Affix postage stamps to the letter for the correct postage and Recorded Delivery fee.
4 Hand this certificate, together with the letter, to an officer of The Post Office.
5 This certificate will be date-stamped and initialled as a receipt. Please keep it safely, and produce it in the event of a claim.

Name

Address

Postcode

Recorded Delivery should not be used for sending money or valuable items.

For Post Office use   Date stamp

Accepting Officer's initials

Recorded Delivery no.

P2297 Apr 84

Parcels

Postage rates
Local/non-local postage rates apply to all inland parcels. Cost depends on whether the addressee is within the defined local area or not, and on weight.

Compensation Fee (CF) Parcels
These are handled along with all other inland parcels but an additional fee covers compensation for loss or damage.

Fig. 4.6   Compensation Fee parcel form

The Post Office
Certificate of Posting for Compensation Fee Parcel

How to post
1 Enter below in ink the name and full address as written on the parcel.
2 Tick the appropriate box at the bottom of the form to indicate the compensation cover required.

Name

Address

Postcode

Stamps for Compensation Fee (to be cancelled by accepting officer)	For Post Office use
	COD Deposit/ Inpayment Document No
	Compensation Fee Paid
	p Accepting Officer's initials

Date stamp

Tick compensation cover required

Up to £60 ☐
Up to £125 ☐
Up to £225 ☐
Up to £350 ☐

PP89 Feb 84

Postage Forward Parcels.
A Post Office licence is required by a business wishing to use this service. Preprinted return address labels must be provided to customers and the addressee is charged postage and a fee.

Rider Services
A new range of services is being developed for local business operating in areas where an overnight collection and delivery service is needed. Initial services include Nightrider in London.

Trakback

This is a new signed delivery service for parcel contract holders. Verbal confirmation of delivery, normally five days after posting, and a copy of the recipient's signature are available as extras. A bar-coded label is attached to each parcel, which is sent through the ordinary parcel system. Upon signed delivery the bar-code is read into a computer. Confirmation of delivery is made by a free call to the Trakback Response Centre.

Fig. 4.7   Trakback logo

4.2   Royal Mail International Services

All-Up

There is one class of mail for letters to Europe. The rates charged are those for surface mail outside this area. The items are sent by air whenever this results in earlier delivery, but Air Mail labels and stationery are not required. Advantageous postal rates apply for mail to EEC countries.

Printed paper

Specific items classed as printed paper may be sent by the All-Up service or travel by sea at special printed paper and small packets rates, when special packing is necessary.

Airstream

This is a new worldwide letter service for customers sending more than 2 kg of mail per collection. Financial savings are offered to large users.

Express Overseas

Items travel with the ordinary mail to the delivery office, from where they may be taken by messenger. A fee is payable in addition to postage. This service is not available to all countries but includes parcels, letters and printed paper.

Swiftair

This is an express postal service for air mail letters, printed paper and small packets to all countries. Items receive special UK handling and express delivery abroad. Items must carry a Swiftair label as directed and may be registered or insured. Delivery should be made one day earlier than ordinary services.

Fig. 4.8   Swiftair label

International Business Reply Service

Overseas clients are encouraged to reply to UK companies without incurring postal expenses. Unstamped preprinted station-ery is provided by the UK company and postal charges are met by them for each reply received. This new service is currently available to many European countries, when the All-Up service is used. This service will be extended to other countries.

International Reply Coupons

These can be bought from the Post Office and sent abroad to be exchanged for postage stamps in the customer's own country. This allows prepayment for replies at surface mail minimum letter rate.

International Datapost

This is a fast courier service to over 80 countries. There is a free money-back guarantee in case of delay and a free loss, damage and consequential loss insurance.

Intelpost

This is a large electronic service, using facsimile equipment to transmit copies of documents to centres throughout the world. Documents may be collected from the customer's premises or delivered to a major Post Office. Alternatively, a customer may transmit from their own facsimile, telex or microcomputer equipment to an Intelpost centre when an addressee does not have compatible equipment. A receiving centre may deliver documents the same day or items may be collected from centres. When the addressee is a facsimile, telex or computer user, items can be routed to their private terminals. Cost depends on the number of pages, destination and method of delivery.

4.3   Additional Post Office Services

Discount services

Direct Mail
Several services are available to companies frequently posting large quantities of letters or packets. A generous introductory discount is available for first time users and the service may be combined with the Freepost or Business Reply Service.

First/Second Class Letter Contracts
These are offered for mailing 5000 or more presorted items at any one time.

Bulk Rebate Service
Discounts are available for more than 4250 presorted Second Class items which are of the same shape, size and weight. Delivery may be up to seven working days after posting.

Prepayment
This can be arranged for a large number of items posted in one day.

Miscellaneous services

Poste Restante
Post may be addressed to an individual or company at a Post Office, from which it is then collected.

Selectapost
A company may have the mail sorted, perhaps into departments, by the Post Office prior to delivery.

Private box
A company may hire a private box (or bag). Mail may be collected by the company at their convenience instead of waiting for the Post Office delivery.

Cash on delivery
Various parcel and packet services can be combined with this service. The Post Office will collect payment for the sender to a

maximum of £350 on an enclosed invoice. Amounts over £50 must be paid on Post Office premises. It is also available to certain foreign countries.

Late posting facility
Registered and Recorded Delivery items are accepted on travelling Post Offices.

Redirection
Mail may be directed to another address for up to twelve months on payment of a fee.

Special Search
On payment of a small fee, the Post Office will search for an item at the delivery office.

Reference material

Post Office Guide
This annual publication is kept up-to-date with supplements and gives comprehensive details of prices, weight/size limits and information on all Post Office services, both inland and abroad.

Leaflets
Many leaflets are available from Post Offices giving details of individual services.

4.4   Alternative Express Services

Red Star/Night Star
Most main line railway stations have a Red Star office. Parcels may be handed in or collected and put on the first available train to a destination station. From there they may be delivered or collected. This is a quick, 24-hour or overnight service. It is also available to some European centres. Details are available from Red Star offices.

Fig. 4.9   Red Star/Night Star logo

Questions

1   What is the Poste Restante service and who is most likely to use it?
2   Give two examples of the types of business which would benefit by using the Business Reply Service or Freepost.
3   Which service would you use to ensure a letter of application for a job would be delivered the next day?
4   Why is it not necessary to put Air Mail labels on letters to Europe?
5   Which service would you use to return exam certificates to an applicant for a job?
6   Visit your nearest Red Star office and ask about the services available.
7   Use the Post Office Guide to calculate the amount of postage due on the following items:

1 parcel (local)	24 kg
1 parcel (national rate)	16 kg
6 2nd class letters	41 g
1 1st class letter	85 g
10 letters 1st class	55 g
100 circulars 2nd class	45 g
6 samples 2nd class	112 g
1 letter Special Delivery	75 g

Chapter 5

Telecommunications

Telecommunication services and the range of equipment available in the United Kingdom and worldwide have all increased rapidly. Advances in electronics and the use of satellites and fibre optics have made communications easier and quicker. The facilities now available with electronic equipment are wide and varied.

5.1 Telephones

Switchboards

PMBX (Private manual branch exchange)
This is a system in which all incoming and outgoing calls are handled by the operator. Employees may dial external numbers after the operator has connected them to a line on the switchboard. Internal calls are usually on a separate system.

PABX (Private automatic branch exchange)
This is a system in which incoming calls are handled by the operator. Outgoing calls can be dialled from a handset after obtaining an external line by dialling one digit. Internal calls are dialled direct.

CALL-CONNECT
Electronic systems are now widely used and whilst the switchboard and handset models vary, the facilities usually include:

Call logging: A record can be kept of all outgoing calls from each extension, with length of time and details of numbers dialled. A print-out can be obtained.

Call diversion: Incoming calls can be diverted automatically to another extension when the line is busy, if there is no reply or for all calls.

Call back: Internal calls can be reactivated if the line is busy or the call unanswered.

Call transfer: Calls can be transferred to another extension.

Conference call: Up to seven parties can be connected by an extension user or the operator.

Call barring: Any extension can be prevented from making unauthorised calls, usually external calls, and in some cases from receiving incoming calls.

Extension group hunting: Extensions are arranged in groups and incoming calls are routed to a free extension in the group.

Abbreviated dialling: Most electronic phones will store numbers and these are activated by use of a short code number.

Automatic redialling: If a number is engaged it can be automatically recalled by the use of one key.

System X

BT have started to replace their exchange equipment with this new electronic equipment which will speed up communications and allow the introduction of many new services. Speech and data can be connected concurrently or a call changed from one to the other. This integrated digital system allows customers to be connected to advanced network services including electronic mail, telex, facsimile, electronic fund transfer, teletext and viewdata, graphics and slow scan TV.

Answering calls

If a switchboard operator has not already given the name of the company before passing the call to you, state the company name first. Then state your name or department. Avoid all casual expressions such as 'Hello'. Keep a pad and pen by the telephone to write messages down as they are given and read them back to the caller before ending the conversation. If there is likely to be a delay while you find information or another person, suggest that you ring the caller back rather than leave them holding on. If you do keep someone on the line, go back to them frequently to apologise for the delay so they do not think you have forgotten them.

It is important to develop a consistently cheerful and welcoming tone however busy you are. Address the caller by name when you can.

Fig. 5.1   Message form

Making a call

Before picking up the receiver, ensure you have the number in front of you and that you know for whom to ask and what you wish to say. Dial carefully and listen for the ringing tone. When the call is answered state your name and to whom you wish to speak. If you are connected to a wrong number, apologise and try again.

Telephone answering machines

This equipment is similar to a tape recorder and is sometimes combined with the handset. The telephone line is interrupted and

Fig. 5.2   A telephone answering machine

a prerecorded message is played to the caller, who can usually leave a message. These machines are widely used by small businesses where the office may be unattended and in larger companies for enquiry services or to avoid frequent interruptions. Calls can be answered 24 hours a day, so covering the worldwide time differences. A remote control 'interrogator' can be used from any telephone to replay messages, clear the tape, add an additional message and reset the machine.

Radiophones

There are networks which allow calls to be made from and received by mobile telephones. These are mostly used for business and may be installed in trains, cars or boats.Calls can be made to places abroad, ships and oil platforms in coastal waters. There is a recorded data service for weather, motoring, etc.

Cellphones

A large number of small areas (cells) have been organised to serve customers with mobile phones. The handsets are battery-powered and fit into a briefcase, allowing them to be used anywhere. Additional facilities include memory, conference calls and call transfer.

Cordless phones

These are mobile handsets which require a base unit connected to the telephone line. They are useful for people who move around their workplace.

Ships' radiotelephones

Calls may be made to ships at sea via satellite, Coast Radio Station or Phonetex, a message dictation service via Portishead Radio.

Skyphones

Telephones are being installed in some planes to enable airline passengers to make in-flight calls to anywhere worldwide, paying by credit card. Incoming calls to the aircraft cannot yet be received.

Radiopaging

Radiopaging devices are available for private company systems and from BT on their national system. Several styles are available from pagers which alert only by bleeping to the devices which also display visual data. The group call can alert up to 99 pagers from one telephone call. There are radiopaging centres and service points throughout the country. There is a bureau service and direct input from the office telex or datel link to those with visual display. Message link is a mailbox facility whereby messages can be stored and retrieved.

Fig. 5.3   A radiopager

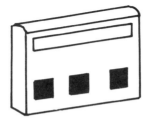

5.2   Telephone Services

ADC

This advice of duration and charge service can be requested from the operator, who connects the call and then calls back to tell you the cost.

Personal calls

This service enables a caller to specify the person to whom he wishes to speak and the charge starts when the two people are connected. If the person called is not available the operator will leave a message and will attempt to complete the connection during the following 24 hours.

Fixed time calls

A call may be booked in advance at a convenient time. Prior arrangement with the recipient will ensure that he or she is available.

Information services

BT provide many information services for personal and business use including sport and leisure data and:

    FT Cityline—financial data updated seven times a day
    Traveline—rail, road, air and sea information
    Weatherline—local weather forecasts
    Timeline—the 'speaking clock'.

Non-cash services

Freefone

This service is free to the caller who asks the operator for the Freefone number or name. The recipient is charged a fee and the cost of the call. This is a valuable service for enquiries from potential customers.

Phonecards

Cards can be purchased at airports, post offices and shops then used instead of cash in special payphones.

Fig. 5.4   A phonecard

Credit call

Calls are made through the operator and charged to individual telephone credit card numbers. Charges are listed on the telephone account.

Account call

A special code is entered and the cost is listed on the telephone bill.

Linkline

This service is designed for advertisers of many goods and services and may be used by the customer free or at the cost of a local call. The remainder of any charge is met by the Linkline subscriber. International Linkline allows customers abroad to call the UK free of charge, the cost being met by the receiving subscriber.

5.3   Telecommunication Services

Telex

This is the public teleprinter service run by BT which is fast and accurate. Subscribers to the service rent equipment which can send and receive messages through the telecommunication lines; messages are printed on both sending and receiving equipment simultaneously. It is a 24 hour international service and charges are based on time and distance. To speed up transmission time most older equipment can prepare and read paper tape. Modern electronic equipment has a visual display unit on which the message can be prepared before sending. This equipment can be programmed to send stored messages when lines are clearer and cheaper, i.e. overnight, and all teleprinters can receive messages whilst unattended. It is most useful when discussion is not necessary, for written confirmation of business, statistics, foreign languages, urgent information and to cope with international time differences. A telex message is usually acceptable as legal evidence. The teleprinter is very easy to use and a directory of numbers and answerback codes is produced every six months.

The TextDirect service enables users to access the Telex service through word processors, personal computers and some electronic typewriters.

The BT Telex Plus service offers:

Store and Forward—messages sent when lines are free; repeated attempts made if necessary.

Multi-address—up to 100 addresses worldwide.

Prerecorded addresses—up to 100 addresses listed on the computer and activated by a confidential code.

Packet Switchstream—electronic terminals can connect into services such as Teletex.

Private company teleprinter systems also exist for communication between the sites of one firm.

Telemessages

Telemessage® is a BT electronic mail service available via the operator from any telephone up to 10 pm (7 pm Sunday). Messages may also be sent through telex, Prestel, Dialcom or the customer's computer terminal. The message is transferred to the Royal Mail sorting office nearest the destination, printed and delivered by post on the next working day. There is a minimum charge up to 50 words and attractive stationery is available for most special occasions. There is a multi-address facility for business users and a discount on 'same text' messages.

Fig. 5.5   Telemessage logo

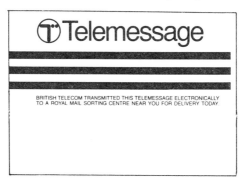

International Telemessages

The telemessage service is available to the USA.

Telegrams

International telegrams may be sent by telephone via the operator or by telex. They are available worldwide and cost depends on distance and length of message.

Confravision

This is a public sound and vision conference service connecting eight studios around Britain. Business can be conducted as if the people were face-to-face but it saves the time and expense of travel and hotels.

Videostream

An international videoconference service is now available in the UK and internationally by satellite, so people thousands of miles apart can hold a meeting.

A portable terminal is also being developed to enable users to operate from their own premises instead of travelling to studios.

Teletex/electronic mail

There are international electronic mail services for sending messages between terminals, which may be electronic typewriters with adapter, electronic telephone exchanges or computers. Data can be transmitted directly from the office computer or word processor to similar equipment via the telephone network within the company or through the BT Teletex service. Teletex can be linked with telex but this requires special equipment as it is 30 times faster than the telex system. Terminals can send and receive messages without disturbing message preparation. Repeated attempts to connect are made if necessary and messages are sent memory-to-memory so they can be prepared, stored and sent, then stored, read and printed if desired. Each terminal has a unique identity for security and each message identifies the sender and records the date and time.

Telecom Gold

This is a BT electronic mail system compatible with the worldwide Dialcom electronic mail system. Each subscriber has a unique mailbox in which incoming messages are stored but which only he can access. Most computer equipment can be used as a terminal, with a modem coupler and a standard telephone line. Private user groups operate within the system and it is connected to the telex and radiopaging services. Many information services are also available on databases, e.g. airline data and credit control.

Datel

Data can be transmitted directly to and from computers by means of BT's Datel services. Keyboards, printers, modems, VDUs and card and tape equipment are used. International Datel services operate via the telephone and telex lines.

Bureaufax

This is a British Telecom facsimile bureau service linked to the Royal Mail Intelpost system. (See Section 4.2).

Imtran

Telephone conversation is linked to still television pictures for advice and decision-making at a distance. It is useful for doctors, architects, engineers and other experts who can look at a diagram or photograph and hold a discussion.

Videotex

This title encompasses two data systems:

Teletext
Television channels are used to transmit information. Using a keypad the viewer can call a page of data on to the screen. Ceefax and Oracle are the UK one-way systems provided by the BBC and IBA. Viewers cannot communicate with the system. (See Section **13.3**.)

Viewdata
Private systems can operate within an organisation giving information relevant to their work. The public UK system is Prestel available to business and individuals. A Prestel set or microcomputer linked by modem to the telephone line is used to access the system and each subscriber has a number and password. As it is a two-way system subscribers can receive and send information, make hotel, travel and theatre reservations and buy goods.

There are a number of 'closed user' groups on the Prestel service to which members subscribe to receive data or communicate with each other. (See Section **13.3**.)

5.4   Integration

Whilst each piece of electronic equipment can be bought and used separately, progress is rapidly being made to unite them into a fully integrated system. This would enable the same equipment to be used as a terminal for all the services and for the terminals to communicate directly with each other.

Questions

1   Describe the following telephone facilities:
    extension group hunting
    call barring
    call logging
2   What do the following terms mean:
    ADC   PABX   SYSTEM X
3   How does the Freefone service operate and who is most likely
    to use it?
4   What is a phonecard and where can you obtain one?
5   How might a business benefit from installing an answering
    machine?
6   What is electronic mail?
7   How might you send a telex message from your office desk?

Chapter 6

Receiving Visitors

The skills involved in receiving visitors are mostly the same in private and working life, but whilst private life has become more casual, this aspect of business life is usually still very formal. The reception area is often the first part of a company with which a potential customer has direct contact, creating a first impression which forms his/her concept of the company and which can influence the business relationship. The receptionist is consequently the first employee met by a visitor and he/she is therefore an ambassador for the employer.

In an efficiently-run and well-organised company, the receptionist receives a list of expected visitors in advance from other employees such as secretaries. This helps her to prepare for these visitors and often she can greet them by name, which always gives a good impression. When a visitor comes in and gives his/her name, she will also know whether or not he/she is expected. She might also be given the names of unwanted guests, in which case she need not waste her time enquiring for someone to see them. It is important, of course, to make all visitors feel important and welcome and to treat them all equally.

6.1 Reception Duties

The procedure to be followed when an appointment has been made:

— greet the visitor with 'Good morning/afternoon' and add their name if this is known;
— complete the visitors' register, (see Fig. 6.1);
— ask the visitor to sit down whilst you inform the contact of their arrival;
— telephone the contact and follow their instructions to keep the visitor in reception or arrange an escort to the office.

40

Fig. 6.1 Example of a visitors' book

Date	Visitor's Name	Company Name	Arrived	Departed	Contact
7/2/88	J Smith	A . B.S .	09·45	10.30	R Soams
7/2/88	P.M'Laughlin	Keypoint	09.55	11·00	S.Haste .

You should not:

— allow a visitor to walk around unescorted, however well they are known;
— leave a visitor sitting for a long time without acknowledgement. Apologise for any delay and perhaps offer a cup of coffee. (Many reception areas now have drinks machines.)

If the visitor does not have an appointment, it may not be convenient for them to see the individual for whom they ask. They should be offered the opportunity to:

— make an appointment;
— see someone else;
— wait, given an indication of the time involved;
— leave a message.

Sometimes it is necessary to be very firm (but always polite) with a persistent visitor who wishes to wait or who keeps calling without an appointment.

A receptionist should keep well-classified details of firms and contacts. This can be compiled from the visitors' register and visiting cards. These records can be used for follow-up contacts and may form a mailing list for company literature—in which case incorrect or incomplete details could result in loss of business.

Figure 6.2 Business/Visiting Card

Many receptionists have to undertake a variety of other duties, which may include: telephone switchboard, typing, clerical work, arranging meetings, booking rooms, etc. Clear priorities need to be laid down in order not to annoy visitors and lose their custom.

Additional duties are also involved in specialist reception work, such as medical and dental, personnel departments, hotels, and temporary reception duties for conferences and other functions.

6.2   Security

Many companies are becoming increasingly security conscious. As a part of their procedure they issue visitors' passes or security tags for which the receptionist is responsible. The plastic tags usually clip to clothing and a pass can be checked by an employee. These items are retrieved when the visitor departs.

6.3   Personal Qualities

It is important for a receptionist to have a wide knowledge of company organisation and work. This can minimise frustration to visitors and the waste of employees' time.

The most important personal qualities needed to handle situations which might arise would be:

tact/diplomacy	punctuality
patience	loyalty
firmness	reliability
courtesy	neat appearance
even-temperament	

6.4   Dealing with the Press

Many companies have a clear policy on handling visitors from the Press or media. This may mean that:

— they are seen only by prior appointment;
— the subject of the inquiry must be known beforehand, or a list of questions presented;
— a particular employee (i.e. Press Officer) is responsible for all contacts;
— statements are made only in writing to avoid misquotes.

All other employees must avoid answering questions or giving any information or opinion, regardless of the persistence of the journalist.

6.5 Reception Area

Most companies appreciate the importance of carefully siting their reception area for security and to avoid visitors bypassing it.

Generally, reception areas are given high priority in terms of decor and furniture to ensure that they create a favourable impression and are welcoming and comfortable.

The layout should be carefully planned to ensure the receptionist is in a position to see everyone who comes in. Points which require attention are:

— attractive, well-maintained decor, including carpet and curtains or blinds;
— comfortable chairs for waiting visitors;
— attractive and appropriate furniture;
— plants and pictures;
— company literature and/or appropriate journals;
— availability of hot/cold drinks;
— uncluttered surroundings;
— receptionist's name displayed on the desk;
— well-presented, smiling receptionist.

Questions

1   List the personal qualities needed by a receptionist.
2   How should you respond to a journalist calling into reception without an appointment?
3   How can a secretary help a receptionist to perform her duties efficiently?

Chapter 7

Written Communication

In an office information is passed on through internal and external channels of communication involving a variety of documents.

7.1   House Style

Managers appreciate the importance of the appearance of external documents and many companies issue guidelines to employees to ensure uniformity of display. Instructions may be given regarding layout, signature blocks, paper sizes, the production and distribution of copies, etc. Documents produced for special events such as conferences will usually carry the company logo and be presented in the house style.

7.2   Composition of Letters

Care must be exercised in composing letters to ensure they convey the correct tone and message, and they should be displayed in an accurate and attractive way. Avoid long confusing sentences and do not stray from the point you wish to make.

There must be an introductory paragraph, making reference to the subject matter or to an earlier communication:

'We thank you for your letter of 18 May, concerning delivery of your order No 14732.'

'I refer to our telephone conversation of yesterday concerning your training programme.'

The message is developed or questions posed or answered in the middle paragraph(s). Some information may also be tabulated, i.e. list of items/prices/dates. Always check that you have omitted nothing or delay may result.

44

'We have pleasure in enclosing a copy of our latest brochure and price list. We should like to draw your attention to . . .'

A final paragraph should state what action is then expected, e.g. payment within a stated time, receipt of an order or an appointment arranged.

'We look forward to hearing from you . . .'

Circular letters

When an organisation wishes to send the same document to a number of people a circular letter may be produced. This document has the same house style layout as an individual letter but may not be addressed to individuals by name, for instance: Dear Customer, Dear Member, etc. A master sheet may be prepared and printed, into which names and addresses can be inserted later by typewriter or addressing machine, or the mail merge facility on a word processor. This gives an 'individual' letter appearance. If a reply is required, a tear-off portion may be provided at the foot of the letter.

Standard form letters

When a company sends a similar letter to many people, but the information varies, a standard letter may be produced with space left for later insertion of details. Production of the letter would be the same as for the circular.

Word processors have also increased the use of standard paragraphs. An individual document can be compiled by combining any of the paragraphs stored on the system. This system has largely superseded the production of form letters and ensures the use of standardised wording as part of the house style. It saves much time in initial composition and in the production of the most frequently used documents.

7.3   Writing a Memorandum

Companies usually provide printed memo forms which follow their house style. The information can be typed or handwritten with a subject heading but in a less formal style than letters. A memo may be signed or initialled, but is often sent unsigned, and copies may be taken if desired. In some companies memos have been superseded by electronic messages. (See Electronic mail, Section 5.3.)

7.4   Displaying an Effective Notice

A notice should demand attention by making an impact, with the most important points highlighted. The message needs to be short but complete, and carries a signature if appropriate.

Noticeboards should be maintained neatly, retaining only current information. A large board may be divided into clearly labelled sections to aid clarity.

7.5   Bulletins

A bulletin is a short report on an event or current situation often restricted to one subject. Employees may be given a copy or it may be posted on a noticeboard.

7.6   House Journals

Many companies produce a booklet for employees. It is intended to give relevant company information to foster an atmosphere of cohesion and co-operation between management and employees, or between sites or branches. It usually includes details on current discussions, sales achievements, long-service awards, sporting activities and suggestion scheme news, often with photographs. Depending on the budget available, this journal may be a colourful, glossy magazine or be presented in newspaper style.

7.7   Newsletters

A regular paper may be compiled and sent to each employee, giving information of interest from management. It may give similar information to the house journal but it does not usually include photographs or colour printing and is cheaper to produce.

7.8   Telex Messages

As telex messages travel through the telecommunication lines, the cost of transmission depends on the time and distance involved. It is therefore necessary to keep the message reasonably brief, especially if it is being sent directly from the keyboard. Special numbers and abbreviated addresses are used to reduce the length of a message. Ensure that every part of the message is clear and any unnecessary description or explanation is omitted. A follow-up letter may be sent to confirm the telex and give more detail if necessary. (See Section 5.3.)

7.9   Telemessages

This message service replaced internal telegrams some years ago. As there is a minimum cost for up to 50 words, it is not necessary to be unduly brief. As with telex, the message should be carefully planned to ensure that it is complete and clear. Explanation or description which is not essential may be given in a follow-up document. (See Section **5.3**.)

7.10   Presenting a Report

Many reports are produced in the course of running a business. They are generally compiled:

— after a study by committee or working party;
— for consideration/decision by committee or management;
— to record the proceedings and discussion of a conference;
— to record research/product developments;
— to give expert advice;
— as a record of a business trip or exhibition.

Written reports vary considerably in length and complexity. Some may be short, requiring only a few paragraphs or the completion of a form, whilst others take many pages and contain much detail.

All lengthy reports should be carefully prepared, using headings, tables and diagrams where helpful to the readers. The main components should be:

— a title page or heading;
— terms of reference, stating the reasons for and limitations of the report;
— investigation or presentation of information, in clearly defined sections;
— findings or analysis of information;
— conclusions reached;
— recommendations or suggestions for action;
— appendices giving additional detail, if needed;
— signature block and date.

7.11   Summaries

In order to minimise the large amount of reading required of managers, and to convey the main details briefly, a summary of a report, article or series of correspondence may be produced.

The main document must be read thoroughly several times to be fully understood. Each section is then studied to select the principal points and a draft summary compiled, using your own words where appropriate. Check this carefully against the original(s) for accuracy. Ensure the summary is complete and conveys the correct message. Retain names and technical data but omit detailed descriptions and repetition from the original(s). Details of the main document(s), i.e. date, author and title, should be added for reference. The final summary is then produced in the past tense, with appropriate paragraphing.

7.12   Invitations and Replies

Most executives receive invitations to a variety of functions. These may be contained in a letter, but frequently are formal in style and wording.

Fig. 7.1   A formal invitation

The Directors of Kumfy Furniture

request the company of

Mr Michael Taplow

at the opening of their new showrooms

410 London Road, New Town

at 11.30 am on Tuesday 23 February 19..

RSVP
Ms R Roberts
Personnel Manager

Buffet Lunch

A reply should follow the style of the invitation, so a letter of acceptance/refusal may be sent replying to an original letter. A formal reply should follow a formal invitation, when much of the wording can be 'lifted' from the original.

Fig. 7.2   An invitation acceptance

```
        Mr Michael Taplow has pleasure in

     accepting the kind invitation of the

     Directors of Kumfy Furniture to the

     opening of their new showrooms at

  410 London Road, New Town at 11.30 am on

          Tuesday 23 February 19..


96 Grange Road
New Town
```

Fig. 7.3   An invitation refusal

```
     Major and Mrs William Featherstone regret

     that they are unable to accept the kind

     invitation of the Directors of Kumfy

     Furniture to the opening of their new

     showrooms at 410 London Road, New Town on

            Tuesday 23 February 19..




23 George Street
New Town
```

Questions

1   Your employers, Travel Tours of Bridge Street, Eastbury, who arrange package holidays, have just been informed that two of the new hotels in Majorca which were to be used during the coming season will not be completed in time; there have been difficulties with the supply of building materials and a long spell of wet weather has delayed the work. There are not sufficient vacancies in other hotels and clients can accept an alternative holiday or cancellation with full refund.

   (*a*) Compose a circular letter to your clients whose holiday bookings are affected.

   (*b*) Compose a telex message to be transmitted to Mr Black, your representative in Majorca, informing him that your Tours Manager, Mr White, will be flying out to meet him on 24 March. Whilst there, he wishes to meet representatives of the builders—perhaps Mr Black would arrange a meeting on the 25 March—he also hopes to inspect the hotels which are unfinished. Mr Black is also to arrange this. Mr White will stay for three days and will need accommodation.

2   Reply to this invitation:

Major D J MacDonald-Hunter

requests the pleasure of the company of

MR & MRS P T BEAUMONT

for luncheon at 12 noon

on Sunday 21 February 19--

86 Long Lane
New Town   *RSVP*

Chapter 8

Visual Aids

Statistical data can be more easily and quickly understood by presentation in chart or graph form rather than in a table.

These charts and graphs may often be presented as part of a report or displayed on wall boards, at exhibitions, etc. Preparation by hand can be very time-consuming and changes cause delays. It is now quick and easy to prepare these diagrams with the aid of a computer program.

It is necessary to consider the final method of presentation when preparing the diagrams. The use of colour adds interest and aids rapid interpretation of the data, but where it is not possible to produce the colours a variety of shading styles must be used. Always give a key to the colours or shading used and state the scale on the graph.

8.1   Line Graphs

These are used to show a wide range of statistics, i.e. sales/profit figures, temperatures, wage levels, etc. The graph may show only one line, but often has several lines representing similar information for comparison, e.g. performance of branches, sales of different products. The line graph is particularly suitable for showing fluctuations and trends.

Example

Using the figures below showing sales totals for three branches, a line graph (see Fig. 8.1) can be produced:

	Brighton	Swindon	Bristol		Brighton	Swindon	Bristol
January	25300	29600	24000	July	44000	38800	26000
February	34000	30200	23600	August	38500	37500	27500
March	38200	32800	28000	September	38200	37200	27800
April	40600	34600	29600	October	36900	36600	25500
May	42800	36400	25800	November	34800	35000	25200
June	45000	38600	24800	December	32000	33500	24500

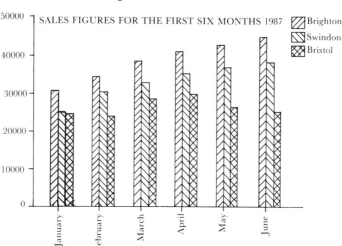

Fig. 8.1 A line graph

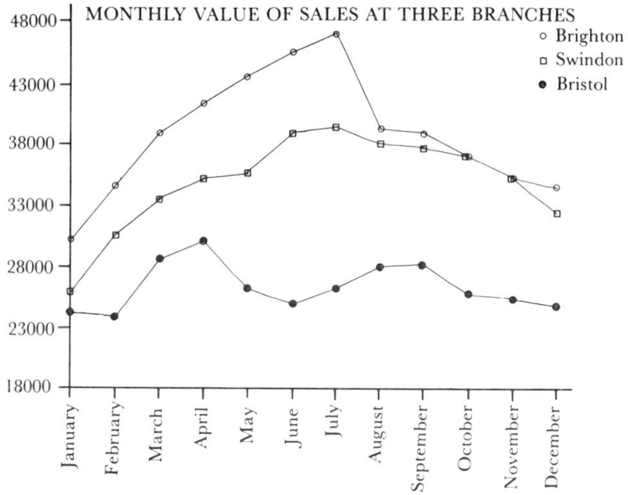

MONTHLY VALUE OF SALES AT THREE BRANCHES

- ○ Brighton
- □ Swindon
- ● Bristol

8.2 Bar Charts

Bar charts can display the same information as a line graph, using either vertical or horizontal bars instead of lines. They are most useful for contrasting data over a short period of time. It is advisable to limit the chart to three or four bars per period otherwise it becomes confusing to the reader.

Example
Using the figures from Figure 8.1 for the first six months, a bar chart can be produced:

Fig. 8.2 A bar chart

SALES FIGURES FOR THE FIRST SIX MONTHS 1987

- ▨ Brighton
- ◨ Swindon
- ▧ Bristol

8.3   Sector Charts

It is possible to show the same type of information on one bar, using different styles of shading. This is a sector chart. However, if too many sectors are incorporated it can be difficult to interpret the data quickly.

Example
Taking the figures for the second half of the year in Figure 8.1, a sector chart can be produced:

Fig. 8.3   A sector chart

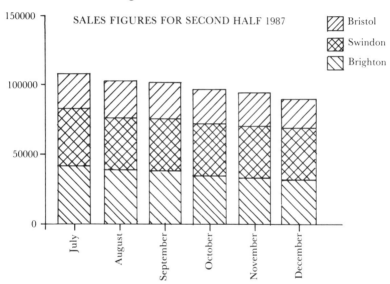

8.4   Pictograms

The horizontal bars of a chart may be built up by using a picture to represent the figures, e.g. one car to represent 100 000 output, one sack to represent 100 tons of grain. This style of chart is particularly attractive at exhibitions or on screen, but is not appropriate in company reports.

8.5   Z Charts

This is a specialised line graph which is built up month by month to show three items—monthly total, cumulative total for the year to date and the moving annual total. The name derives from the shape made by these three lines. It is most useful for recording financial or sales data and showing fluctuations and trends which assist forecasting and planning. Comparisons can be made with previous years and between months and seasons.

Example

Using a company's sales figures below, a Z chart could be produced at the end of December 1987 showing:

	Monthly	Cumulative	Moving Annual
January	50	50	585
February	45	95	600
March	40	135	600
April	45	180	600
May	60	240	605
June	65	305	610
July	60	365	605
August	70	435	615
September	60	495	630
October	55	550	635
November	45	595	635
December	35	630	630

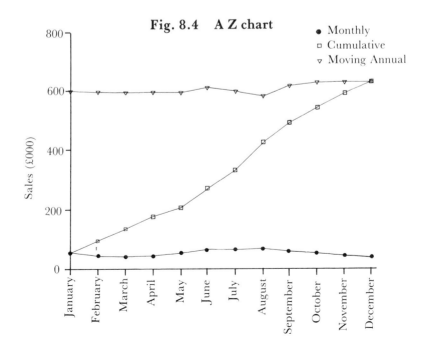

Fig. 8.4   A Z chart

8.6 Break-Even Charts

A company needs to know the level of output at which their costs equal their income. This is the break-even point, below which a loss occurs and above which increasing profits are made. A break-even chart is another specialised line graph.

Example

A company's costs and revenue can be plotted to show the break-even point and level of profit or loss (Fig. 8.5):

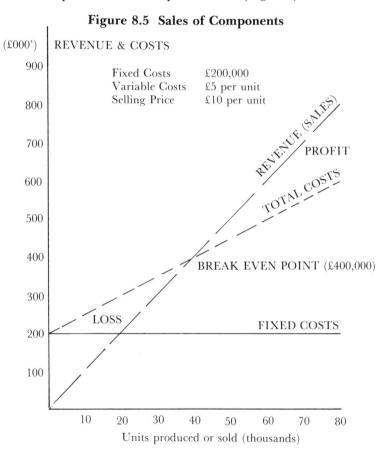

Figure 8.5 Sales of Components

8.7 Gantt Charts

This is a horizontal bar chart which is usually used to compare expected progress/achievement with actual achievement. It is used to plan and control work flow and output. It also assists accurate costing of work.

Example

The planned time scale on a given project can be indicated with the actual time taken shown against it (Fig. 8.6):

Fig. 8.6   A Gantt chart

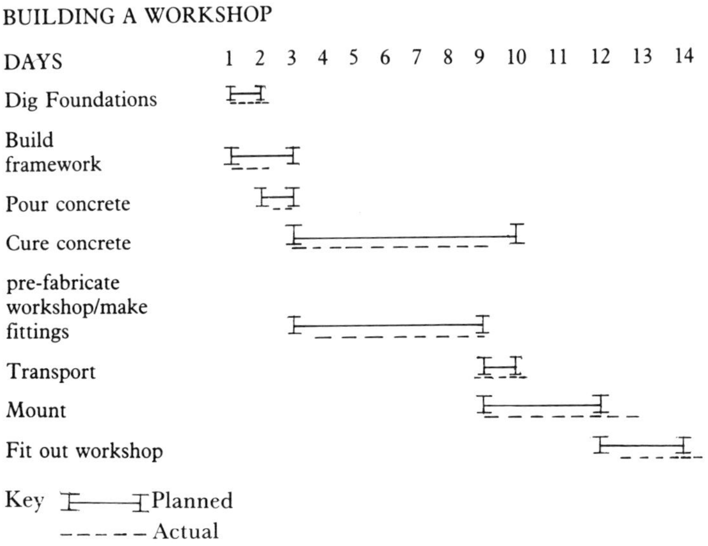

BUILDING A WORKSHOP

DAYS	1 2 3 4 5 6 7 8 9 10 11 12 13 14

Dig Foundations

Build framework

Pour concrete

Cure concrete

pre-fabricate workshop/make fittings

Transport

Mount

Fit out workshop

Key ⊢━━━⊣ Planned
      ─ ─ ─ ─ Actual

8.8   Pie Charts

This chart derives its name from its circular shape which is divided into sections representing the figures. The whole circle represents 100% and the sections can be quite accurately drawn to represent the parts making up the whole. This chart is most suited to displaying percentages and proportions.

Example

Here pie charts are used to compare the percentage of time spent on various activities in a traditional office and one using a word processing system.

ANALYSIS OF TYPING TIME

	Traditional	With WP System
New work	25	65
Retyping/correcting	35	15
Paper handling	13	5
Other work	22	10
Personal	5	5

Fig. 8.7 Pie charts

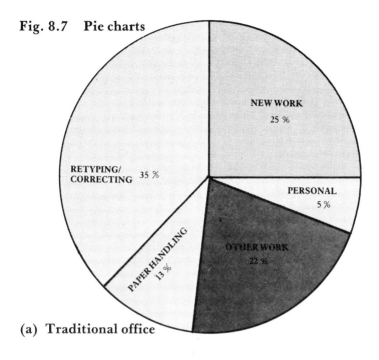

(a) Traditional office

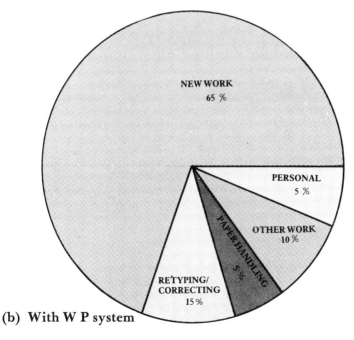

(b) With W P system

8.9   Flow Charts

A flow chart is a diagram which represents a sequence of activities, operations or events. It gives a clear and simple visual present-ation which might otherwise take many words to describe. Examples of simple flow charts are used in Figures 3.1 and 3.5 to represent the incoming and outgoing post handling procedures. Flow charts are very helpful in various types of analytical work and they are widely used in work study (Organisation and Methods) and computer operations (Systems Analysis).

In this work a number of specially shaped symbols are used to represent each type of activity or operation. Additional informa-tion is provided by text which is usually written inside the symbol. The symbols are connected by lines or arrows clearly indicating the flow of activity. Wording may be added to these lines to convey extra information. For example, when a decision is required *Yes/No* may be written beside the line. The most commonly used symbols are shown in Figure 8.8.

Fig. 8.8   Flow Chart Symbols

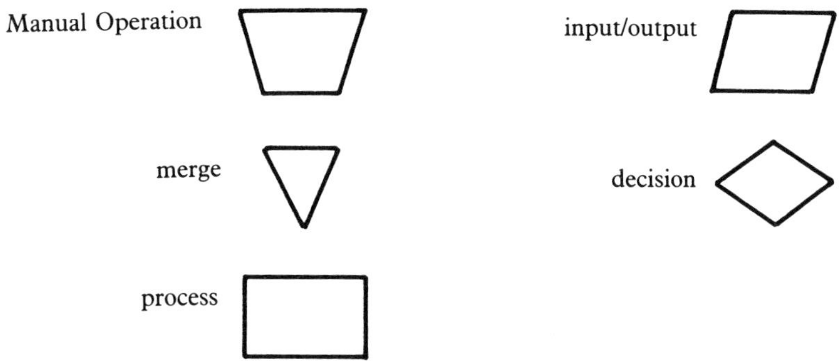

Manual Operation

input/output

merge

decision

process

8.10   Visual Planning/Control Boards

All forms of charts and graphs can also be presented on wall boards for use in the office and at exhibitions and conferences. Boards may be plain or preprinted with a grid, calendar, map, etc. for long-term use.

White board

This has a white laminated surface on which felt pens are used and which is easily cleaned. Electronic white boards can produce photocopies of what has been drawn on them.

Magnetic board

The metal surface of the board is magnetised to retain a variety of symbols and shapes. The surface may be white to give it a dual role.

Year planner

This is a grid showing the months and days of the year for planning work, holiday rotas, etc. A perpetual version is printed on a magnetic board, but paper annual planners are available quite cheaply from stationers and there is a fiscal version (April-March).

Pin board

A soft, dense board for posting notices with drawing pins is useful in many situations.

Peg board

On this board there is a grid of small holes over the surface, into which special lettering and symbols fit. It is useful for information which frequently changes, e.g. menus, hotel/conference centre directions.

Questions

1 Name the three items of information shown on a Z chart.
2 What type of data is a pie chart most suited to represent?
3 Draw a line graph using the following turnover figures:

(£000)

	Manchester	Sheffield	Plymouth
Jan	620	400	420
Feb	640	405	410
Mar	650	410	425
April	710	425	450
May	725	440	475
June	740	420	485

4 Draw a bar chart using the figures in Question 3.
5 What type of wall boards would be most useful at a conference and what type of information would you expect to display?

Chapter 9

Meetings

It is said that some executives spend 40% or more of their time in meetings. Many meetings are small and informal, that is they are mostly unplanned and undocumented. They arise from daily issues and may involve discussion and/or decision-making, in which case a memo, notice or instruction may result.

Formal meetings are generally pre-planned, carefully documented and follow recognised procedures. They are held at all levels of an organisation and by clubs and societies for briefing, reporting and decision-making. They are an essential part of communication and co-ordination inside and outside an organisation.

9.1   Types of Business Meeting

Annual General Meetings

The Company's Act 1980 dictates that a company's Board of Directors meet the shareholders at least once a year. Reports are made, director appointments may be ratified and votes taken on other issues.

Extraordinary (Special) General Meetings

If an urgent matter arises, or at the request of a number of shareholders, additional meetings between shareholders and the Board may be held.

Board meetings

The directors of an organisation meet to decide policy and discuss company business.

Executive meetings

A variety of committees exist within the management of an organisation to control the business. They may be Standing (permanent) or Ad hoc (temporary, for a given purpose). Some have specified decision-making authority, while others are purely advisory and report to a higher committee.

Co-ordination meetings

Representatives of the various departments, or branches, of a company meet regularly for discussion, advice and decision-making.

Briefing meetings

Managers hold meetings with representatives of the employees within their departments to pass on instructions.

Consultation meetings

Regular meetings are held between representatives of the management and the employees to discuss grievances and problems, when working conditions are the main concern.

9.2 Documents

Notice of Meeting

This is a short note stating the committee title, time, date and place of the next meeting which is sent by the secretary. It is often combined with the agenda.

Agenda

This is a list of the business to be discussed at the meeting, compiled by the Chairman and sent out by the secretary. Certain items are standard, i.e:

1 Apologies for absence
2 Minutes of last meeting
3 Matters arising from the minutes

Some committees also have:

4 Correspondence.

Special items are then listed and the agenda ends with 'Any other business' and, if necessary, 'Date of next meeting'.

Fig. 9.1   Notice of meeting and agenda

WORDLINE RECREATIONAL COMMITTEE

The next meeting of the Recreational Committee will be held in
the Pavilion Committee Room on Wednesday 24 February 19..

AGENDA

1   Apologies for Absence

2   Minutes of the Last Meeting

3   Matters Arising from the Minutes

4   Correspondence

5   Subscriptions

6   Theatre Outing

7   Tennis Matches

8   Any Other Business

9   Date of Next Meeting

J Harrison   12 February 19..
Hon Secretary

Fig. 9.2   Chairman, Agenda

WORDLINE RECREATIONAL COMMITTEE

The next meeting of the Recreational Committee will be held in
the Pavilion Committee Room on Wednesday 24 February 19..

CHAIRMAN'S AGENDA

1	Apologies for Absence	1
2	Minutes of the Last Meeting	2
3	Matters Arising from the Minutes	3
4	Correspondence	4
5	Subscriptions	5
6	Theatre Outing	6
7	Tennis Matches	7
8	Any Other Business	8
9	Date of Next Meeting	9

J Harrison   12 February 19..
Hon Secretary

Fig. 9.3   A G M agenda

```
WORDLINE RECREATION SOCIETY

ANNUAL GENERAL MEETING 17 MARCH 19..

AGENDA

1       Apologies for absence

2       Minutes of previous AGM held on 18 March 19..

3       Matters arising

4       Secretary's report

5       Treasurer's report and adoption of audited accounts

6       Vote of Thanks to retiring Officers

7       Election of: President

                     Chairman

                     Deputy Chairman

                     Vice Chairman

                     Treasurer

                     Secretary

                     Membership Secretary

                     Social Secretary

8       Election of Honorary Auditors

9       Any Other Business

J Harrison                              16 February 19..
Hon Secretary
```

Minutes

These are a record of the main discussion, decisions and voting which occurred during a meeting and are normally written in the third person by the secretary, then approved by the Chairman. They may be entered in a Minute Book or duplicated and distributed to members. They follow the order of the agenda and their accuracy is approved at the following meeting.

Fig. 9.4   Minutes

MINUTES OF WORDLINE RECREATIONAL COMMITTEE HELD IN THE PAVILION COMMITTEE ROOM ON WEDNESDAY 24 FEBRUARY 19..

PRESENT: W Blake (Chairman)
S Carter
J Harrison
P Martin
R Pollard
Miss M Swanson

1 APOLOGIES FOR ABSENCE

Apologies were received from Miss C Cartwright.

2 MINUTES OF THE LAST MEETING

The minutes had been circulated so they were taken as read. There being no amendments, they were duly signed.

3 MATTERS ARISING

Tennis Courts: The work on relining the courts was complete and the fencing had been repaired.

4 CORRESPONDENCE

A letter had been sent to convey the Club's thanks to the Northway Garden Centre for the prizes they donated to our snooker competition.

5 SUBSCRIPTIONS

Following an increase in expenses a discussion took place on increasing subscription rates. It was decided to defer this matter until the Annual General Meeting when full discussion would be held with the members.

6 THEATRE OUTING

The recent theatre outing to a comedy in London was a great success. After discussion it was agreed that another trip would be organised in the Autumn to a musical. Mr Martin agreed to make enquiries about block booking and coach prices.

7 TENNIS MATCHES

Some discussion took place concerning the timing and frequency of tennis matches.   Last year some members complained that the courts were too heavily used and they were unable to play as often as they wished. It was agreed that league matches must continue but the friendly inter-club meetings would be limited to four in the season. These would take place on a Tuesday evening and as much notice as possible would be given.

8 ANY OTHER BUSINESS

Mr Harrison questioned the age limits on tennis club membership, which were confirmed as:

Juniors   - up to 15
Intermediates - 16-18
Adults   - 19 and over

9 DATE OF NEXT MEETING

The next meeting was arranged for 31 March 19 ..

Signed .... Date ....

Minutes can be presented in several ways. The agenda item is usually used as a heading. A column to record the initials or names of people required to take action on points in the minutes can be very helpful. They are numbered, either exactly as the agenda or by a predetermined system, e.g. 34/87 this being a topic number combined with the year. Each time a topic is discussed during that year it retains the same item number. This aids retrieval but requires an alphabetical index of topics with meeting dates.

9.3 Duties of the Chairman

It is important that a chairman is well prepared for each meeting. He is responsible for ensuring that the business is conducted fairly and abides by the rules and procedures laid down in the terms of reference (Articles of Association, Standing Orders or Constitution).

He must gain the respect of the members to generate their co-operation. He must see that all members have the opportunity to speak and that no member dominates any discussion. He should ensure the discussion remains relevant and that members do not hold private conversations at the same time. It is usual for the Chairman to present an impartial summary of discussion before a vote is taken. He retains overall responsibility for the administrative and financial matters, which are delegated to the secretary and treasurer respectively, and he may give instructions to them or request information from them.

9.4 Duties of the Secretary

It usually falls to the secretary to prepare (with the Chairman) and distribute all the documents for the meeting and handle the correspondence concerning the committee's work. The secretary keeps records, including the Attendance Register and notes apologies from absent members. He/she is responsible for the detailed arrangements for meetings, such as booking the room and refreshments, preparing and clearing the room. During each meeting the secretary should sit beside the Chairman to take instructions and provide support as required. He/she takes notes from which the minutes are drafted for the Chairman's approval.

9.5 Glossary of Terms

Listed on the pages that follow are the main terms used in connection with meetings.

Ad hoc

This term is used with reference to a committee (or sometimes a meeting), which is constituted for a particular purpose. When the business is completed the committee is dissolved.

Addendum

This is an amendment to a motion which adds to the wording, perhaps to clarify or limit its effect. Voting on an addendum is separate to that of the motion.

Adjournment

After a meeting has begun the chairman, with the members' agreement, may put off the rest of the business until another time. Adequate notice of the reconvened meeting must be given and the same agenda is continued. An adjournment is called if time is short, tempers are disrupting business, the number of members present drops below quorum, or more information is needed for decision-making.

Agenda

This is a numbered list of points for discussion at a meeting, usually taken in number order. However, the Chairman may agree to take an item out of order by special request.

AGM

This is the Annual General Meeting when management reports to the shareholders.

Amendment

This is a proposal to alter the wording of a motion.

Articles of Association

These are the rules by which a company is run, which will generally include the constitution and conduct of committees.

Casting vote

The Chairman is usually allowed a second vote which is used only when there is an equal number of votes for and against a motion.

Co-opted

Members of a committee may vote to co-opt a person on to the committee as an extra member, particularly for his expertise.

Ex officio

This refers to a person who is a member of a committee 'by virtue of his office' (position) within the company, i.e. a Head of Department can attend all Section meetings.

Honorary

An office held without salary or fee is an honorary one, and is usually that of Secretary or Treasurer.

In attendance

Persons attending a meeting who are not committee members are recorded in the minutes as being 'in attendance'.

Intra vires

This term is used of a function or decision within the power of the person or committee concerned.

Lie on the table

If the members do not wish to drop a motion, but cannot make a decision at the meeting, the matter is left open and may be included in a later meeting.

Motion

A carefully worded, written proposal given to the Chairman for discussion by the committee. The 'proposer' speaks first, followed by the 'seconder'. When put to the committee it becomes 'the question' and after discussion the proposer can speak again. If approved on voting, the motion becomes a 'resolution'.

Nem con (nemine contradicente)

When no votes are cast against a motion, but it is not unanimous as some members abstained, the motion is passed 'nem con'.

Out of order

If the procedures are not according to the rules, then an item or a member can be ruled 'out of order'.

Point of order

If a member thinks the rules are not being followed he can raise a 'point of order', when the rules will be checked and a decision made.

Postponement

A meeting which has not been started, may be put off to a later date. Adequate notice of the postponed meeting must be given and, if desired, a new agenda may be produced. This may be due to a more urgent matter arising or to lack of a quorum indicated by the apologies for absence received in advance of the meeting time.

Proxy

This is a person (usually another member) authorised to attend a meeting and vote for an absent member. He has a document called the 'instrument of proxy' which also records the member's wishes.

Quorum

This is the minimum number of persons who must attend a meeting to make it valid and any decisions binding. This number is given in the rules and varies between committees.

Resolution

When a motion has been approved it becomes a resolution and is binding on the committee.

Rider

A rider is extra wording added to a resolution after it has been passed. The rider must be proposed, seconded and put to a vote.

Sine die

This refers to an adjournment for which no time or date is given for continuation of the business, i.e. the adjournment is indefinite.

Standing orders

These are the rules by which an organisation or society should be run. Also called the Constitution.

Ultra vires

This term is used of a function or decision outside the power of the person or committee concerned.

Unanimous

A motion is unanimous when all members present vote for it, with no abstentions.

Questions

1 List the duties of a committee secretary.
2 What are minutes of a meeting and who prepares them?
3 List the arrangements to be made before a meeting.
4 Explain these terms in relation to meetings:

ad hoc	quorum
ex officio	co-opted
proxy	casting vote.

5 What is the difference between:

postpone and adjourn
unanimous and nem con
motion and resolution?

Chapter 10

Record Keeping

In business, information is retained for several reasons:

— to comply with legal requirements;
— to provide a history of the company's business;
— as proof of decisions made;
— as a record of transactions undertaken.

It is essential that all records are kept in an orderly fashion so that the information is readily available and easily understood by all. It is also most important that records are kept up-to-date.

10.1 Centralised Records

It is common for one filing department to service the whole company. This is usually run by a supervisor, with clerks who have a comprehensive knowledge of the system and a wide understanding of the company's work and organisation.

Only one file is maintained for each topic, so minimising the amount of paper retained and 'the space required for storage. Confidential material, i.e. personnel files, policy documents, etc. needs greater security and would not generally be kept in a centralised system.

It usually takes a little longer to retrieve information from a centralised system than from one's own office files. As computerised systems become available throughout a company, each office employee has immediate access to the information required and delays are minimal.

10.2 Decentralised Records

When each section or individual manager keeps a separate filing system this leads to much duplication, involves more equipment, space and expense. It is, however, more convenient for the employees and this system would be used when frequent reference is necessary.

10.3   Filing Equipment

Most papers are retained in manilla folders with bulky documents/ catalogues in box files. A small system, particularly suitable for travellers, is the expanding folder.

In the office files are kept in metal cabinets (usually lockable) to give the greatest protection from fire damage. The most common are:

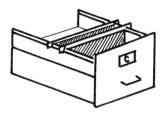

Fig. 10.1   Vertical

Vertical

Files are placed in suspension pockets in a cabinet of two, three or four drawers. Only one drawer should be opened at any one time to avoid accidents. Always close drawers immediately after use.

Fig. 10.2   Vertical

Lateral

Open shelves or lockable cabinets can hold many files in suspension pockets. They can go above eye level, unlike the vertical system, and so hold more files in the same floor area.

Fig. 10.3   Lateral

Rotary

A small system may be contained on a rotary holder. This is not lockable but can be housed in an alcove. If in the open, it may be used by several people at one time.

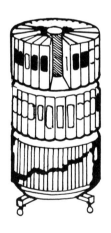

Fig. 10.4   Rotary

Fig. 10.5   Plan chest

Plan chest/cabinet

Large documents, e.g. posters and plans, may be kept in a large chest of shallow drawers or suspended by holders in a cabinet, a smaller version of which is used for duplicator stencils or OHP transparencies.

Fig. 10.6   Plan cabinet

Electronic cabinets/systems

Each cabinet has a keypad and the files are arranged on runners. The user taps out the file number required on the keypad of the cabinet and within a few seconds the file is placed in front of him.

10.4   Card Holders

Where only a small amount of information is involved this may be recorded on a card and retained in a card holder.

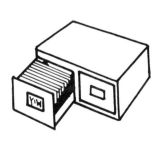

Drawers

A series of small drawers retain cards in a vertical position.

Fig. 10.7   Drawers

Visible edge

Shallow trays hold the cards flat in overlapping holders exposing the edge of each to form an index, without other details being visible.

Fig. 10.8   Visible edge

Rotary

A small desktop stand holds the cards. It can be rotated to bring the required card to the top.

Fig. 10.9   Rotary

Wheel

Many cards can be kept on a wheel which turns in a horizontal plane.

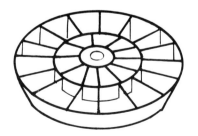

Fig. 10.10   Wheel

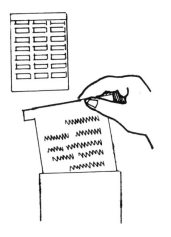

Fig. 10.11 Slot index

Slot index

A wall board with many slots can retain T-shaped cards, displaying the top of each for quick location.

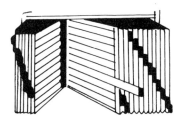

Fig. 10.12 Strip index

Strip index

A single line of information can be recorded on individual strips of card and placed in the runners on a prepared board. The strips are easily inserted or removed. They can be arranged in any order and rearranged without retyping. This is useful for a telephone index, production data etc.

Edge-punched cards

Each card has a series of holes around the edge representing specific information. Slots are cut at the required points and when a steel needle is passed through the holes the slotted cards fall out. By repeating the process for each item of information, the relevant cards are found. These can be used by estate agents, or for personnel or production records. They are also available in larger units with runners used instead of a needle.

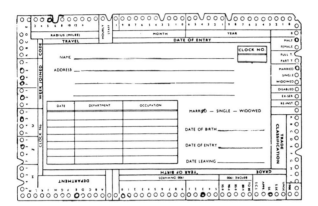

Fig. 10.13

10.5   Classification

Alphabetical

This is a popular method which everyone can understand and which can be easily increased/decreased. It can be used for clients' names, product titles, subject titles, committees and most business documents. Some basic rules are usually necessary to avoid confusion, e.g. how to deal with foreign names or distinguish between similar titles.

Numerical

This is a widely used method, which is easy to expand/contract as required. It is the best method for documents referred to by number, i.e. orders, invoices, etc, and for a centralised system housing a wide variety of documents and subjects. An alphabetical index is necessary for users to check the file number they require.

Alpha-numerical

Some companies employ a mixed reference method which combines letters and figures, but which may require some explanation or simple rules.

Decimal

The Dewey decimal method is a variation of numbering which allocates a figure to a wide subject, e.g. 200 Safety. Sub-divisions are shown by adding a decimal point and another figure, e.g:

200.1 In the office
200.2 In the home
200.3 In the workplace
200.4 Safety equipment
200.5 Safety Committee

Each section can be further subdivided by adding another figure, if desired, e.g. 200.41 Eye protection.

This system is used to categorise books in libraries.

Final digit

Another numbering method which is occasionally used is the final digit system. For example, a file reference may be 214759. This file has a major file division of 59, sub-section 47 and individual file number 21. This is not a straightforward system and unless familiar to an individual it can lead to misfiling, but it also increases security.

Chronological

This method is used within each file but is not generally regarded as appropriate for a complete system. Papers are filed in date order, with the most recent on top.

10.6 Guides

All record systems need to be clearly labelled and primary guides are used to show the major divisions, with secondary guides for sub-dividing large sections. Each file division is also labelled.

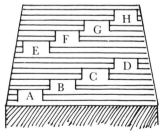

Fig. 10.14

10.7   Colour Codes

It is possible to used coloured files and/or guides to indicate a second important classification. The Personnel Department may file alphabetically by employees' names but use coloured files or guides to show which department they work in, e.g. pink for Sales, green for Purchasing, etc. Stick-on symbols, such as coloured shapes, can be added to denote 'under 18', 'over 60', etc.

10.8   Cross Reference

If a document concerns more than one topic, copies may be made and filed under each title. Otherwise a cross-reference slip should be inserted in the alternative file to assist retrieval.

```
CROSS  REFERENCE  SHEET


DOCUMENT  ENTITLED/
CORRESPONDENCE:




FILED  UNDER:


```

Fig. 10.15

10.9   Out Cards

A record should be kept of files removed from the system so that they can quickly be located. A card may be put in place of the file stating who has taken it, with the date. Some companies prefer to enter the details in a book.

10.10   Follow-up Systems

When a document needs to be reviewed or a reminder given, a follow-up note needs to be made. This can be done in several ways.

A note may be put in the diary, or a follow-up notebook or there may be a follow-up file in which to place the document or note.

There is also the 'tickler' system, which is a series of files or file divisions, labelled from 1 to 31, plus one for each month of the year. Documents for the current month are placed in the numbered sections. If a reminder is required in a subsequent month, the document is placed in the appropriate monthly section. At the end of one month the papers for the next month are transferred to the numbered section to be dealt with on the appropriate day.

10.11   Computer Records

Much information is now stored on computer and word processing files using disc, tape or microfilm. It is important that back-up copies of records are made and stored in a separate place in case of loss or damage. It is also necessary to ensure that back-up copies are kept up-to-date. The data is rapidly accessed, easily read on a VDU and can be printed at each workstation. A centralised system servicing the whole company is usually maintained in the form of a database, so that the information can be used in a variety of ways by employees. Where limited access to data is required it is necessary to have a password.

There is now a digital optical recorder which uses a laser beam to store masses of text on disc, which is very rapidly retrieved.

Data Protection Act 1984

This legislation was introduced to control the use of computers for storing personal information. The Data Protection Registrar was set up and it is an offence if companies concerned do not register. Details required are:

— data held;
— purposes for which used;
— sources of information;
— categories of people to whom data is disclosed;
— foreign countries to which data is transferred.

Data users must adhere to certain principles regarding collection, holding and disclosure of personal data. Subjects on whom data is held have the right to access, to seek correction if data is inaccurate and to claim compensation for damage or distress caused to them.

Exceptions to the Act include data held concerned only with one's own personal, family and household affairs or for recreation purposes.

Microfilm

Documents and computer output are frequently transferred on to film for storage. The film takes only a fraction of the space of the paper documents, which are photographed, the film processed and then viewed using a reader or projector. The film can be produced by an agency but a company must have equipment for reading their films. It is particularly useful for old records to which reference is infrequent, but is now popular for current records in some companies.

If a printed copy is required of any document kept on film, it can be quickly and easily made by a reader with a photocopying facility.

Microfilm has several advantages over paper filing:

— it saves much space and weight, e.g. one film can hold the same as a cabinet drawer;
— the film is less prone to damage than paper and does not deteriorate;
— the film is easily sent through the post.

There are several types of film:

Roll film
This is widely used and is particularly suited to records which are in sequence.

Cartridge
The roll film is protected by a plastic casing and is easier to handle in this form.

Microfiche
This is a sheet of film with rows of pictures, holding the equivalent of many A4 pages on one sheet.

Jackets
Strips of film are held in place on a page. They form a loose-leaf system which can be rearranged or up-dated easily.

Aperture cards
A frame of film is mounted on a computer card punched with information. The card is read electronically.

Edge-punched cards
A frame of film can be mounted on an edge-punched card recording associated information.

Computer output on microfilm (COM)
Data from a computer can be transferred directly on to film at a speed of around 120 000 characters per second. This is quicker than direct printing and the film takes much less storage space.

If a printed copy is required of any document held on film, it can be quickly and easily made by a reader with photocopying facility.

Microfilm has several advantages over paper filing:

— it saves much space and weight, e.g. one film can hold the same as a cabinet drawer;
— the film is less prone to damage than paper and does not deteriorate;
— the film is easily sent through the post.

Questions

1 What is cross-referencing and when would you use it?
2 What is colour coding and how can it be used to aid accurate record-keeping?
3 What are the advantages of alphabetical classification?
4 List the advantages of microfilm over traditional paper filing.
5 What is a database?
6 Place the following people and firms into FOUR geographical areas, listing the names alphabetically within each group.

   Miss G Bates, Gillingham, Kent
   Mr N Morris, Portsmouth, Hants
   Mrs E A Thomas, Preston, Lancs
   S Spencer Esq, Winchester, Hants
   Messrs Hopson & Son, Dover, Kent
   Dr B Jamieson, Canterbury, Kent
   Messrs Hill & Co, Wigan, Lancs
   The Barrington Trading Corporation, Dartmouth, Devon
   Mrs J R Powell, Morecambe, Lancs
   C Morgan & Sons, Exeter, Devon

Chapter 11

Electronic Equipment

After many years of slow change the rapid advance of electronics is being felt in the office. Whilst the main responsibilities of the office staff remain the same, the method of work has often been changed. Material is prepared in a different format for handling by new equipment and the procedures are carried out more efficiently by the machinery.

11.1 Typewriters

Electronic typewriters are rapidly replacing the manual and electric machines which have been in use for so long. They offer the advantage of quiet operation and high quality production, as well as many features not available on the other machines.

Extended keyboard

A greater number of characters are available as some keys can be used in combination with a 'code' function. These include superscript and subscript figures, a degree sign and accents.

Fig. 11.1

A daisywheel

Interchangeable heads

Daisy wheel printing heads are easily changed, extending further the number of characters and range of type styles and sizes, e.g. italics, maths and science symbols, foreign characters.

Print size

The size of characters and use of proportional spacing can be selected from the keyboard in combination with the correct printing head.

Special printing

Automatic highlighting is possible on most machines from the keyboard, i.e. bold, spaced lettering, simultaneous underscore.

Justification

Margins can be justified automatically as text is keyed in and printed.

Wrap-around

The automatic carriage return facility reduces the number of key strokes performed and allows the typist to continue with the text. A hot zone is designated before the right margin and the machine will divide the lines at a space within this zone.

Centring

Lines can be automatically centred between margins or between tabulator stops.

Repeat key

There is a facility to repeat any character on the keyboard.

Maintenance

As there are few moving parts maintenance should be minimal.

Upgrading

Some machines can be expanded to full word processing capability by the addition of a VDU and disc drive.

11.2   Dictating Machines

Dictation equipment is widely used in many offices, the most popular medium being magnetic tape. Portable dictation machines are popular with executives who travel extensively. Other arrangements are:

Tandem

An audio-typist working for several managers has a machine connected to a telephone for dictation and a separate transcribing machine for her own use.

Bank

In a centralised typing or WP service the supervisor may control a bank of several machines connected to the telephone system. She ensures that all the machines are ready for use. When a manager wishes to dictate he calls the correct extension and is automatically connected to a free machine. The supervisor removes recorded material and gives it to an employee in the section, each of whom has transcribing equipment.

Direct link

Dictation is relayed by computerised remote-control directly to the typists. Dictation and transcription can be simultaneous but independent, i.e. the typist is able to transcribe a few seconds behind the dictation. The system stores information about the typists' speed and workload and it directs the dictation to the earliest available person.

Advantages of recorded dictation

The main advantages are:

— it does not take the time of both manager and secretary to do the dictation;
— managers can dictate whilst away from the office;
— there is a saving of labour costs as audio-typists are less expensive than shorthand-typists;

— recorded material can be posted, e.g. from agents to Head Office, for action;
— unfamiliar wording can be replayed whilst poor handwriting makes transcription difficult;
— machines can be used for other purposes—to record lectures, meetings, etc.

Disadvantages of recorded dictation

The major disadvantages are:

— audio-typists are not on hand to answer queries or give details during dictation, e.g. names, dates, unlike during shorthand dictation when the secretary is present;
— there is a loss of personal contact;
— there is a lowering of job satisfaction;
— some managers do not like using the machines and others are poor at dictating;
— the equipment can break down and delay completion of work;
— confidential material is best recorded in shorthand so that it cannot be used by other people.

11.3   Word Processors

There has been a rapid increase in the use of word processors in commerce and industry. A wide range of equipment is available. Some electronic typewriters can be upgraded, microcomputers can be used with a word processing package or a dedicated system may be purchased.

The equipment consists of a keyboard, visual display unit (VDU), disc drive and printer, with a processing unit to control the functions.

Word processing allows greater flexibility in producing documents than typewriting. The memory capacity is much greater, allowing long documents to be retained, retrieved and reused. Editing (correcting and altering) text is easy on the screen and avoids repetitive typing, allowing extensive manipulation of text and producing perfect copies. Complete documents can be saved for reuse, 'standard paragraphs' can be filed to make up any document without retyping and merging of files is simple. The larger systems provide automatic features including indexing and contents listing. Most systems include a spelling check and some allow integration of other computer packages such as graphics, a database or spreadsheet.

Operators are always well advised to keep a second (back up) copy of all recorded material and to index their files for quick retrieval.

In larger companies with several 'workstations' the equipment is usually on a shared logic and/or shared resource network, i.e. they share a central computer and/or printer and hard disc storage. The equipment need not be in the same building. Links can also be made with telecom services providing telex, Prestel, electronic mail and telephone services, international databases, etc. at the workstation.

A word processor is ideally suited to producing:

— high quality documents;
— standard letters such as advertising circulars;
— contracts, agreements, leases, etc. using standard paragraphs;
— invoices, requisitions and forms with layout stored;
— documents which need updating, such as price lists;
— draft documents for editing and final processing, e.g. reports;
— data re-ordered in columns, alphabetical/numerical order, e.g. conference delegate lists, personnel lists, etc.

See *Word Processing* in this series for greater detail on this very important piece of office equipment.

11.4   Microwriter

A microwriter is a small, hand-held machine with a window display and six keys designed around the shape of the hand. The key combinations which produce all the alphabetical and numerical characters, symbols, punctuation marks, formatting, editing, etc. can be learned very quickly. With practice it is much quicker than handwriting. It can store up to 1600 formatted words, about five A4 pages, of text. The stored data can be down-loaded on to the office computer or word processor for further editing, printing, etc. without the need for keying-in. It can also be connected to a wide range of electronic office equipment as it is capable of receiving and transmitting data.

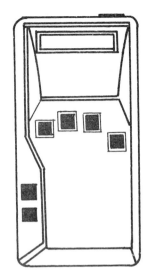

Fig. 11.2
A microwriter

11.5 Facsimile (Fax)

A facsimile machine is an electrostatic copier which scans an original document and sends signals through the telephone lines to a compatible machine which reproduces an exact copy. Photographs, diagrams, tables, signatures and music as well as text can be sent rapidly and accurately. Machines are grouped by their speed and facilities. Group 3 machines are usually compatible with the earlier groups but have additional automatic features such as speed control, line check, paper feed, remote activation and printing phone number, time, etc.

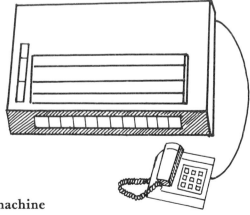

Fig. 11.3
A facsimile machine

The number of machines in use is increasing rapidly, but for firms without compatible equipment there are international bureau services run by Royal Mail (Intelpost) and BT (Bureaufax). (See sections **4.2** and **5.3**.)

11.6   Computers

A computer consists of an input device, a central processing unit (CPU) consisting of arithmetic and control units with a memory capacity, and an output device. There is usually a backing store of additional data. Further remote input and/or output devices may be used offline, i.e. not directly connected to the CPU to allow optimum use of the high speed at which the computer operates.

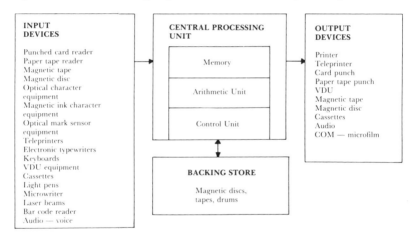

Fig. 11.4

Information processing has advanced very rapidly and computer systems are now available to businesses of all sizes. Individuals and groups of employees in all sections of the office can benefit from the speed and accuracy of computer installations and the additional information which can be obtained. Integrated systems are capable of combining text, data, graphics and design packages.

Office functions

Much of the routine repetitive clerical work previously carried out manually is now performed rapidly by the company computer.

The main office functions for which it is used are noted throughout this book. They include:

  (i) *Payroll*—Programs combine rapid calculation of salaries and wages with updating of records.
 (ii) *Order processing*—Customer order details are fed into computer. The program might include connection with other facilities such as checking stock, producing documents for production.
(iii) *Purchasing/sales records*—Programs store information on customers and suppliers, and retain records of purchase orders.
 (iv) *Stock control*—Programs record movement of stock and outstanding orders, assist in demand forecasts, classify items, carry out up to date costing, warn of danger stock levels, and provide statistics for management.
  (v) *Production control*—Programs assist in efficient scheduling of production and maintenance on all equipment. They can calculate final output and provide statistics for management.
 (vi) *Cash flow control*—Programs record the flow of cash in and out of the business, record overdue debts, assist forecasting.
(vii) *Records storage and retrieval*—A computer can store a great deal of information in a small space which is quickly and easily accessed by employees.
(viii) *Design*—Many programs exist to assist quick and accurate design of many consumer goods, buildings, bridges, etc.
 (ix) *Desktop publishing and advertising*—There is a rapid change from traditional printing methods to computerised typesetting and this is providing a wider range of print styles, graphics, etc.

Networks and configurations

Workstations within a company can be linked to a central computer and to each other by a Local Area Network (LAN). This gives them access to a much greater store of data and a wider range of facilities whilst requiring less storage capacity at each workstation. Groups of employees may share a printer and this would also be more economic. They can be linked worldwide with a Wide Area Network (WAN).

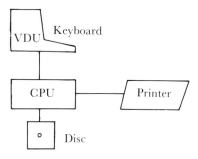

Fig. 11.5   A stand alone system

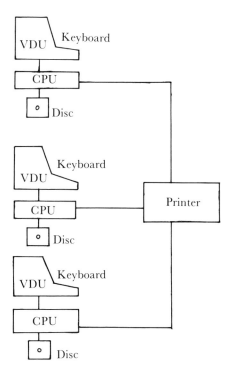

Fig. 11.6   A shared resource system

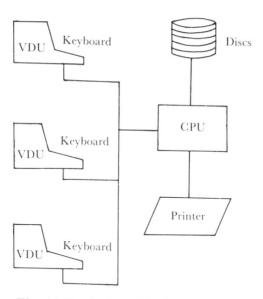

Fig. 11.7   A shared logic system

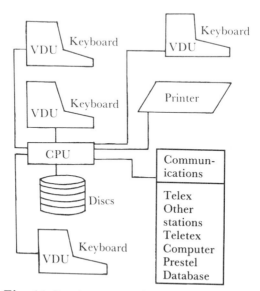

Fig. 11.8   A communication system

11.7   Printers

There are a number of printers used for computer data output. As they mostly work more slowly than the central processing unit, they are often 'offline', that is they are not directly connected to the CPU. The data is stored by a different means, i.e. on paper tape or magnetic disc, and off-loaded to the separate printer. There are several types of printer:

Daisy wheel

These printers use the same style of head as many electronic typewriters and produce a good quality print-out but work quite slowly, 55 cps (characters per second). They may be used for text, when the head can be changed to provide different type styles. They cannot handle graphics.

Dot matrix

This is a very popular type of printer. The print head consists of a number of pins which form the character shapes. They are faster than daisy-wheel machines, up to 250 cps with bi-directional printing. Quality may be varied from draft to near letter quality (NLQ) on most machines by repeated striking but this slows down the output.

Ink jet

There is no printing head to touch the paper surface. Characters are formed by a fine ink jet sprayed on to the paper and absorbed. Excellent quality of print is obtained and the output is fairly fast, i.e. 100 cps.

Laser

When a document is sent from the computer to the printer, a picture of the whole page is built up in the printer's memory. The image is transferred to a light-sensitive drum which holds a positive electrical charge. The laser light scans the rotating drum, transferring the picture in its memory on to the drum by neutralising all the points where an image occurs. When the drum passes through the toner powder this sticks to the neutralised areas and is rejected by other areas on the drum. The picture is transferred to paper and is fused by heat.

The printer produces copies with the highest quality print of any image—text, graphics, etc.

Questions

1   What additional features are available on an electronic typewriter rather than an electric machine?
2   Describe a bank dictation system. Where is this system most likely to be installed?
3   List the advantages of recorded dictation over copy typing and shorthand dictation.
4   Word processors are replacing typewriters in many offices. Explain why.
5   Name the parts of a computer and list as many input and output devices as possible.
6   List the office procedures for which a computer is most often used.

Chapter 12

Reprography

Whilst carbon copies of documents are still made in some companies, the use of copying equipment has expanded rapidly. Many of the slower processes have disappeared in favour of the easy-to-use copying machines. The following machines are those most commonly used.

12.1   Electrostatic Copier

These copiers range from desktop models to large high-production machines and are used in all types of business. Libraries usually have a machine and there are also many High Street 'print shops' who base their work on the larger models. Machines may be rented or bought and companies usually have a maintenance contract for quick service. No specialist training is required for these copiers.

The machine produces an exact copy from any original and some machines will copy on to transparency film. They are clean and quick to use. The more modern machines have many facilities. Warning lights when paper or toner levels are low are common. Paper may be manually fed or contained in one or more trays. Some models will print on both sides of the sheet and handle paper of different sizes. It is possible to enlarge or reduce the image and programme the machine for the number of copies required. Automatic feeding of originals and collating of copies are other features available. Printing on paper of different weights and colours is simple and a range of ink colours is available, i.e. red, green, blue and brown.

Machines which reproduce several colours at once are available but their cost is high and they are not in general office use. When colour is important for a particular task a company would probably use a bureau service. Specialist printing and publishing companies are using these copiers instead of the more traditional preparation methods. Some instruction in their use is necessary.

Electrostatic copiers fall into two categories:

Plain paper

The image is projected on to an electrically charged, selenium-coated roller which attracts powdered ink. It is then offset on to plain paper and fused by heat.

Sensitised paper

The image is directly reflected on to specially coated paper. It is electrostatically charged and fused by heat or pressure.

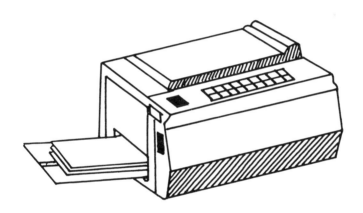

Fig. 12.1   An electrostatic copier

12.2   Dyeline (Diazo) Copier

This machine produces large copies and is the most popular copier for plans and drawings. It uses a roll of light-sensitive, diazo-coated paper which is fed in with the single-sided translucent original. These are exposed to light which bleaches the paper where no image appears. Then the copy paper is passed through chemical or vapour to develop the positive image. Whilst the 'blue print' is the most widely used, other colours are available. This is a relatively slow but inexpensive process. No specialist training is needed to use this machine, but a demonstration is advisable.

12.3   Duplicators

Spirit

Spirit duplicators are not popular in the business world and are rarely found in the office situation. Copy quality is not high and is variable. The image fades gradually in daylight. Where this machine is available it is mostly used to produce a small number of short-term documents such as agendas. Whilst no specialist training is needed, a demonstration is advisable.

Ink/stencil

This electric machine is also far less popular than it used to be but is still used in some offices.

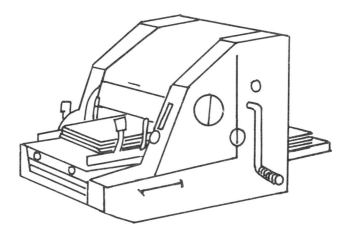

Fig. 12.2   Ink/stencil duplicator

The master is a stencil which consists of a set comprising a waxed sheet, carbon paper and backing sheet. The information is typed without using a ribbon or handwritten using a stylus directly on to the wax surface. They may also be made on a heat copier or an electronic scanner. Special correcting liquid is used to paint over errors and corrections are typed or written over it. The carbon and backing sheet are discarded when the waxed sheet is placed face down on the roller. Absorbent copy paper is placed on the tray and as the roller turns ink is pumped through the cuts in the wax and transferred on to the paper.

Copies are permanent, of reasonable quality and may be printed on both sides of the sheet. Up to 1000 can be produced from an average master. To produce a document in more than one colour, a separate master is needed for each ink colour. When a change of ink is required the machine must be completely cleaned and the drum or ink tube replaced. This can be a time-consuming and messy process.

To retain a stencil for reuse, it should be taken from the machine and blotted to remove the excess ink. It should hang from a rail in the storage cabinet with an index label attached for quick retrieval. Very little training is required to use this machine as most of the process is automatic.

12.4   Heat Copier

This desktop copier relies on heat to produce single copies. The original sheet is passed into the machine with a sheet of heat sensitive copy paper and exposed to a heat source. The original image must contain carbon which absorbs heat and transfers this heat to the copy paper, forming the image. Copies are made singly and are of poor quality but the machine is useful for the other functions it performs. It will prepare masters for spirit and ink duplicating, and transparencies for the overhead projector. It will also laminate, that is it fuses a sheet of plastic to the paper or card to be used for a notice, report cover, etc. Some instruction on the use of this machine avoids wastage of paper due to incorrect temperature setting.

12.5   Dual Spectrum Copier

To overcome the problem of copying non-carbon images by the heat process this machine was developed. The original is exposed to light, together with a transfer sheet. The transfer sheet is then passed through the same process as the heat copier. As with the heat copier, instruction is necessary to ensure acceptable results.

12.6   Colour Transfer

A desktop thermal machine is now available which enables untrained office staff to convert black and white electrostatic copies and laser prints to colour. The finished quality is equal to litho print or foil blocking standard and the process is dry, permanent and very quick. The equipment also laminates paper and thin card in a glossy protective film. Larger machines are capable of thermal binding up to 40 pages in a cover. Overhead projector transparencies can be produced by applying self-adhesive shapes to a sheet of the translucent film. The self-adhesive sheets can be applied to a variety of surfaces to produce artwork for a range of uses. Training in the use of this machine is also minimal.

12.7 Offset Litho Printer

This is a printing process which produces excellent quality copies on paper or card at high speed. A plate is made from the original using either an electrostatic copy, paper or embossed metal. Up to 2000 copies can be obtained from paper and electrostatic plates and 50000 from metal plates, making it possible for companies to print their own letterheads and forms.

The system is based on the principle that oil and water do not mix. The plate is placed around the top roller and as it rotates it comes into contact with the damping and inking rollers. Where the plate is clear it is dampened and where there is an image oil-based ink is retained. This ink is transferred as a mirror image on to the 'blanket' covering the lower roller. It is then transferred on to the copy paper, which is pressed against the blanket by the pressure roller underneath.

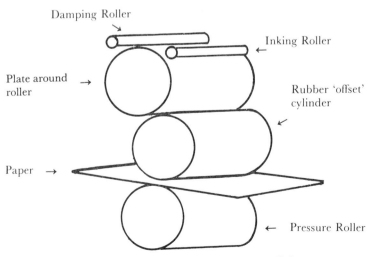

Fig. 12.3   The principle of offset litho

Metal plates may be reused many times and require storage but paper plates are not usually retained. Specialist training in the use of this machine is essential.

12.8 Electronic Scanner

A special carbon stencil is placed on the cylinder alongside the original. A photocell scans the original as the cylinder rotates and where it finds an image a stylus cuts into the stencil reproducing it. The density of scanning can be varied and an A4 stencil can be produced in a few minutes.

Whilst this process is largely automatic, special training is required in the operation and cleaning of this machine. Expert staff, therefore, are usually employed.

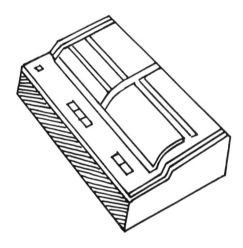

Fig. 12.4   Electronic scanner

Questions

1   Which copier would you use to produce copies of architectural drawings?
2   Which machine would you use to produce 10 000 letters for an advertising mailshot? Explain the reasons for your choice.
3   Describe the ways in which a stencil can be produced for use on the ink duplicator.
4   What particular features of the electrostatic copier make it so popular for office use?

Chapter 13

Finding the Facts

Knowing where to find any item of information is a valuable asset. Most office workers have access to company files and databases containing details of customers, suppliers, products, etc. Other information of a less routine nature or on a specialised topic may be found in a variety of ways.

13.1 Telephones/Personal Calls

Much information can be obtained from a telephone call to outside agencies such as government departments. For example, health queries may be addressed to the DHSS, trade and export problems may be answered by the Department of Trade and so on. Telephone calls to individuals such as a doctor are also common and questions relating to a particular country can be directed to the relevant Embassy or High Commission.

Information on a wide range of topics can be obtained from many other sources, e.g. Chamber of Commerce, Industrial Society, travel agencies, Government bookshops, Press information bureaux, Confederation of British Industry and the Central Office of Information.

13.2 Books

A librarian should be consulted for information of an unusual or specialist nature, but every office should keep a basic range of reference books, together with any specialist publications relevant to their business. These should include some of the following.

English language usage

A good dictionary, e.g. Chambers 20th Century Dictionary
Specialist dictionaries e.g. medical, computing, science and technology, shorthand

Roget's Thesaurus of Words and Phrases
Fowler's Modern English Usage, revised by Sir Ernest Gowers

Communication services

Post Office Guide (detailing all services of the Post Office, published annually with supplements as necessary)
British Telecom Users' Guide (details of all BT services)
Telex Directory (lists telex and answerback numbers, published twice a year)
Telephone Directories (copies of other areas available on request from BT)
Yellow Pages Classified Directory

Travel

ABC Guides (separate editions for world airways, rail, coach and bus, and shipping—timetables and details of services, fares, documents required, etc.)
ABC Guide to International Travel (additional reference for documents, health requirements, climate and individual country details and garage details, etc.)
A good world atlas and gazetteer, e.g. Times Atlas of the World
Local directories and local maps, e.g. Thomson, Kelly

Hotels and restaurants

Good Food Guide (published annually by the Consumer Association)
Michelin Guide to Hotels and Restaurants in Great Britain (annual publication of the British Tourist Industry, also includes a gazetteer of areas of interest)
ABC Hotel Guide (supplement to the ABC World Airways Guide)

Trade and industry

Yellow Pages (classified lists of trade and commerce by area)
UK Kompass (British and European registers)
Directory of Directors (list of directors of principal companies)
Directory of British Associations

People

Who's Who and special volumes (outlines of prominent people)
Debrett's Correct Form (forms of address)

Debrett's Peerage and Baronetage (names, etiquette, forms of address, etc.)

Black's Titles and Forms of Address (correct forms of address, order of priority, etc.)

Crockford's Clerical Directory (Anglican clergy list)

Army list, etc.

Government

Hansard (daily verbatim record of Parliamentary business)

Times Guide to the House of Commons (biographies of MPs and candidates)

Year books

There are many specialist year books; the most widely used are:

Stock Exchange Official Year Book (details of securities, etc.)

British Standards Year Book (information and reference numbers of standards)

Statesman's Year Book (data on international organisations and up-to-date data on each country)

General

Books giving a wide variety of national and international data for reference are updated frequently. The most useful selection in the office includes:

Chambers Office Oracle (details of Royal Mail services, business structure and procedures, communications, limited dictionary and useful data)

Whitaker's Almanack (worldwide information on public affairs, government, industry, finance, commerce, arts, etc.)

Pear's Cyclopaedia (wide range of general information and reference material, e.g. public affairs, economics, finance, music, environment, gazetteer)

13.3 Viewdata/Videotex

Prestel

Viewdata services, which give access to data stored on computer, are a valuable source of information. The most well-known service in the UK is British Telecom's Prestel. The equipment consists of a VDU or modified television, a keypad, a modem and a telephone. A menu of the different types of information services is displayed. The subscriber selects the required information on the keypad and it is shown on the screen by page number. A wide range of information is available on over 200 000 pages. This includes travel timetables, share prices, commodity prices, currency exchange rates, business news and Government information. As Prestel is a two-way service, it is possible to communicate with the central computer to reserve hotels, make travel arrangements, and advertise jobs and products.

If a company wants to provide information only to employees or to distribute confidential information to a selected group this can be done by using the Prestel Closed User Group. Only members of the group can access the data. There is also a message service which is similar to sending a telex. The message is stored in the receiver's mailbox and will be retrieved when the addressee checks that facility.

Teletext

This is a broadcast information system similar to Viewdata, displaying information page by page on screen. The BBC service is Ceefax and the ITV service is Oracle. These are receive-only services and so it not possible to communicate with them. The range of information is more limited than Viewdata but is selected from a keypad.

Electronic Yellow Pages (EYP)

EYP is now available in some areas. This service is free of subscription and computer time charges to users.

13.4   Databases

A database is a system in which information is stored in a structured form, usually on a computer system. Information is stored in 'records' and each record consists of a group of items called 'fields'.

There are a number of international databases offering data to subscribers. Some are specialist sources for groups such as doctors and others are for business subscribers. Information is supplied by large companies and frequently updated. Subscribers in Britain telephone the London office and are connected to the appropriate database which may be anywhere in the world. Using their computer screen and keypad they can request data in the same way as using Prestel. Subscribers pay the telephone costs and may incur a fee from the supplying company.

Questions

1   Where would you expect to find:
   (a) the correct way to address the Mayor of your town?
   (b) the times of trains from London to Edinburgh?
   (c) a brief biography of a celebrity?
   (d) the official report of Parliamentary proceedings?
   (e) details of the Royal Mail Swiftair service?
   (f) of which companies a particular person is a director?
   (g) the name of a four-star hotel in Bath?
   (h) the name of the currency used in Peru?
   (i) details of a recommended restaurant in London?

2   To find a synonym would you use:
   (a) a dictionary?
   (b) Fowler's Modern English Usage?
   (c) a dictionary of quotations?
   (d) Roget's Thesaurus?

3   From which sources of reference would you find out:
   (a) an electrician in your town?
   (b) the telex number of a potential customer?
   (c) the population of your town?
   (d) if a visa is required to enter Yugoslavia?
   (e) if any health precautions are necessary when travelling to Turkey?

4   For what type of information would you use the following reference books:
   (a) Roget's Thesaurus?
   (b) Yellow Pages?
   (c) Whitaker's Almanack?

Chapter 14

Stock Control

14.1 Types of Stock

Every business, whether large or small, is involved in keeping reserves of items, i.e. 'stock'. These stocks may include:

— raw materials or components awaiting manufacture;
— spare parts for machinery and vehicle maintenance;
— finished goods awaiting sale or distribution: stock-in-trade, e.g. goods purchased by a shop for resale:
— consumable items, e.g. stationery, required in the course of conducting the business.

Holding items in stock requires storage space and ties up capital, both of which may cause inconvenience or hardship to the company. It is therefore essential that the use of both space and capital is closely monitored.

14.2 Stock Records

An accurate record of the stock level of each item is essential to ensure that the supply does not run out, causing production to be stopped or administration delayed. Records are also necessary to maintain security on items which are attractive to thieves, and to avoid loss of capital resulting from items 'vanishing'.

A convenient method of keeping stock records is to have a card for each item in the stock room or cupboard. These can be filed by the item description or number, and can include the position on the stock for quick location. A typical example is shown in Figure 14.1.

Fig. 14.1   A stock record card

STOCK RECORD CARD						
Item _BOND A4 WHITE 85GSM_			Max Stock _50 REAMS_			
Location in Store _ _ CR21 _ _ _			Min Stock _20 REAMS_			
	RECEIPTS		ISSUES			Balance in Stock
Date	Quantity Received	Invoice Number	Quantity Issued	Reqn Number	Dept	
1/12/87						20
5/12/87	30	A41270				50
7/12/87			15	17174	Resou. ex.	35
12/12/87			10	18095	Sales	25

Minimum stock

This figure needs to be carefully calculated to ensure an economic level is maintained without creating problems. The points to consider are:

(a) Normal delivery time, i.e. delay between ordering and receiving goods.

(b) Quantity used per day/week/month to cover the delivery time.

(c) Whether goods deteriorate or perish during storage.

(d) The space available with the appropriate conditions.

Changes may be made to the minimum level for:

(e) Seasonal demands and variations.

(f) Impending short-term problems in supply or delivery.

Some companies set aside an amount equal to the minimum stock, placing it in a separate bag or box in the store. When this container (known as the 'bin') is opened, a requisition must be issued to initiate a new order.

Maximum stock

Clearly overstocking is uneconomic, as too much space is occupied and goods may deteriorate. If changes are made in production or administrative procedures some items may be scrapped. For example, the use of a particular form may be discontinued and printed stocks are then wasted. The optimum order size could also affect the maximum stock level.

Optimum order size

For convenience a company may decide to place a regular, perhaps monthly, order for an item it requires. However, in order to qualify for a bulk order discount, so reducing the unit cost of the item, it may be more economic to order a larger amount less often, perhaps every six or eight weeks.

In times of expected shortage or industrial unrest it is advisable to increase order size to build up stocks.

Running balance

The current stock level should be calculated and entered in the final column on the record card each time receipts or issues are recorded. This 'running balance' should correspond to the actual amount of stock at any time. When this figure reaches the minimum stock level a requisition should be issued to the Purchasing Department for them to place an order with the supplier. Stock-keepers can make random checks at any time to confirm the figures on the cards correspond with the number of items in stock.

14.3   Office Supplies

There is often one person in each department who is responsible for issuing stationery and other supplies to office workers. A small stock is kept, in good order, in a locked cupboard and should be issued only in response to a signed requisition. Records should be maintained and random physical checks made. Stock can be replenished from the company's main store regularly, or as required, in exchange for a requisition.

Fig. 14.2   An internal requisition form

INTERNAL REQUISITION		
From SALES		
To STORES		Date 7/12/87
Quantity	Description	
10	A4 WHITE BOND 85GSM.	
Signed S. Smith . Authorized S. T. Woods.		

14.4   Inventories

It is still necessary to check the stock physically to confirm the accuracy of the records, to highlight discrepancies and deter pilfering.

Where checking is undertaken once a year, it can be disruptive to trade and problems can go unchecked for a long time. Some companies still suspend trading while staff are taken away from their normal duties to help with the annual stocktaking.

A perpetual, or continuous, inventory is now popular with many companies. Staff check a number of items weekly throughout the year. Items can be checked several times during the year, at irregular intervals. This system uncovers discrepancies more quickly, so initiating an immediate investigation, and acts as a deterrent to stealing. Where the perpetual system is used, the running balance figures may be taken as the true figures of stock at the end of the accounting period to form the basis of the valuation.

14.5   Valuation

When the accurate figure of stock for each item is determined, a monetary value must be calculated. Stock value is important for two reasons:

(i) The gross profit figure in the company accounts includes a figure for stock.
(ii) The price of materials must be known in order to calculate an accurate cost of each job.

There are several methods by which stock value may be determined.

— *Cost price* (the invoice price charged)

— *Current selling price or current valuation* (the price the trader would get at stocktaking time)

— *Average cost price* (where goods are received at different times and prices, an average is calculated)

— *Last price in* (assumes stock is sold in the order it is received, so remaining stock is valued at most recent prices: First In, First Out)

— *Selling price less gross margin* (branches of multiple-stores may not know all prices, but are supplied at selling prices by Head Office. Stock is valued at selling price by the branches and Head Office deduct the gross (profit) margin they had included).

14.6   Computerised Stock Control

Programs are available to allow stock records to be maintained on the company computer, whether large or small. This may be a simple system replacing the record cards with the running balance adjusted automatically when goods are received or issued. A warning may be given when the minimum stock level is reached. On a large system stock control may be a part of the order processing program, where stock is allocated to production jobs, and the stock levels are adjusted and warning given when the minimum level is reached. An order may be initiated by the system. Valuation can be quickly and easily achieved with the aid of a program using the stock control and price records held on the computer store.

Questions

1   What should be considered when setting the minimum stock level of each item?
2   Explain the term 'optimum order size'.
3   What is a 'running balance'?
4   What is stocktaking? Give another name for this process.
5   What advantages does a perpetual inventory offer over the annual system?
6   How might a company decide the value of their stock?
7   Copy the stock record card in Figure 14.1 and enter the following details in date order. Complete the Balance in Stock column:

Item: Correcting ribbons—dry lift off (Olivetti)
Max Stock: 15 boxes
Min Stock: 4 boxes
Location: Third shelf, extreme left

Date	Quantity Received	Invoice Number	Quantity Issued	Reqn Number	Dept	Balance in Stock
1.11.–6	10	23781				14
13.11.–6	10	23836				
2.12.–6	10	23954				
4.11.–6			3	3426	Sales	
5.11.–6			5	2789	Pers	
10.11.–6			1	4687	A/c	
17.11.–6			3	5123	Purch	
24.11.–6			5	1439	Admin	
30.11.–6			2	3436	Sales	

Chapter 15

Sales/Purchasing

It is important that business transactions are communicated in written form. This avoids confusion and provides a record for both the buyer and the seller. Most of these procedures involve the completion of forms, so ensuring that all the important details are included. This chapter details the order of the documents, the information conveyed, the usual number of copies produced and to whom they are sent.

15.1 Requisition

An internal request is sent to the Purchasing Department requesting the goods to be purchased or taken from stock. A copy is retained in the requesting department.

Fig. 15.1   An internal requisition

REQUISITION			
To: Stores/Purchasing Department			
From: Office Services ' Department			
Quantity	Details	Cat No	Price Each
3	Olivetti Printwheel Mikron 15	TO98	
Signed	Head of Department		Date

15.2 Letter of Enquiry

If the request cannot be met from stock the items may be ordered by the Purchasing Department from their usual supplier. If they do not have a regular supplier then an enquiry is sent to two or three firms requesting details of their terms—prices, discounts and delivery time. A copy is kept by the Purchasing Department. The request may be in the style of a letter or form.

Fig. 15.2   A letter of enquiry

STARLIGHT TOURS
94 Victoria Street
NEW TOWN
Herts AE1 3FG

15 December 1987

Cardinal Office Supplies

55 High Street

OLD TOWN

Bucks

FOR ATTENTION: ACCESSORIES MANAGER

Dear Sirs

LETTER OF ENQUIRY

Would you please be kind enough to quote your price and delivery schedule on the following items:

    Olivetti Compatible Printwheel Mikron 15   Ref TO98
    Olivetti Compatible Printwheel Eletto 12   Ref TO17
    Olivetti Easycart Multistrike Ribbon
    Olivetti ET/Lexicon Liftoff Tape (Pk 6)

We should also appreciate receiving a copy of your latest brochure and price list for all office supplies.

We look forward to receiving your quotation shortly.

Yours faithfully

G M Buckton
Chief Buyer

Discounts

Trade discount
This is a reduction in price given as an allowance between traders, or as an agent's profit.

Cash discount

This is a small allowance deducted when payment is made within a given, limited time.

Quantity discount

This is a reduction in unit price which is allowed on large orders.

15.3   Quotation

In reply to the enquiry, interested suppliers will provide a quotation giving the information requested. It may be accompanied by a catalogue and full price list. If the request was for a service rather than the purchase of goods the reply is usually called an estimate. A copy is kept by the supplier's Sales Department.

Fig. 15.3   Quotation

```
                    Q U O T A T I O N.
             CARDINAL  OFFICE  SUPPLIES
                   55 High Street
                   OLD TOWN    Bucks
    Telephone 0908 54321
                                       Telex 8950522

    VAT No 976 1265 33

    Quotation Ref  PW 8721

    Date    20 December 1987

    To:   Starlight Tours
          94 Victoria Street
          NEW TOWN
          Herts    AE1 3FG

          For attention: G M Buckton
    In reply to your enquiry we have pleasure in quoting you for the
    following:

    Olivetti Compatible Printwheel Mikron 15  Ref T098    £16.08
    Olivetti Compatible Printwheel Eletto 12  Ref T017    £16.08
    Olivetti Easycart Multistrike Ribbon                  £13.95
    Olivetti ET/Lexicon Liftoff Tape (Pk 6)               £11.70

    Note:  All prices are excluding VAT (15%) but include delivery.

    Delivery:  Next day
    Trade discount:
    Terms of payment:  30 days net

    We look forward to receiving your order, which will receive our
    immediate attention.
```

The purchaser compares the quotations/estimates received and decides with whom to place the order.

15.4 Order

An order form is the formal request for goods to be supplied and constitutes acceptance of the conditions of trade given with the quotation. It should repeat all the details concerning the items, price, etc.

Fig. 15.4 An order

STARLIGHT TOURS
94 Victoria Street
NEW TOWN
Herts AE1 3FG

Order No: PW3879

O R D E R

To: Cardinal Office Supplies   Date 2 January 1988
55 High Street
OLD TOWN
Bucks

Quantity	Description	Cat No	Price
3	Olivetti Printwheel Mikron 15	TO98	£16.08 ea + VAT 15%

Delivery: Own van
Next day

H V R Brownlow
CHIEF BUYER

15.5   Advice/Delivery Notes

An advice note may be sent from the seller to the purchaser when the goods are despatched by post or rail. If the seller uses his own transport two copies of a delivery note are given to the van driver. He leaves one with the purchaser and brings the other back signed by the recipient. These documents are usually copies of the invoice and state the items, number of packages and delivery details. The goods should be checked against these details before signing.

15.6   Goods Received Note

In a large company an internal form may be sent from the stores or goods received section to notify Purchasing and Accounts Departments that the goods have arrived.

15.7   Invoice

This is a very important document in the procedure. It is sent from the seller to the buyer and states details and prices of items sold,

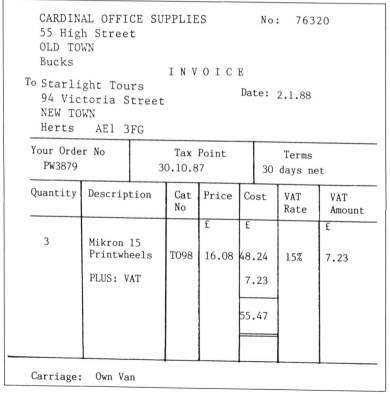

Fig. 15.5   An invoice

including the amount of VAT charged. The number of copies will depend on the size of the company but may include: top copy to purchaser's Accounts Department, and for the seller—one copy for the Accounts Department, one for the Sales Department, one for Transport or Dispatch.

Value Added Tax

This is a tax on most goods and services levied at a standard rate set by the government. Every three months each trader provides details for the Customs and Excise officers stating the tax charged to him and the tax he has charged his customers. He will receive a refund if he has paid out more VAT than he has received, or pay the difference if he has received a greater amount.

The Tax Point, that is the date on which the amount of VAT is calculated on a transaction, is usually the date of the invoice.

15.8   Credit/Debit Notes

If an item is damaged or an overcharging error is made on the invoice, a credit note is issued by the seller. This states the amount, including VAT, which should be deducted from the invoice price.

If an undercharging error or omission is made on the invoice a debit note is issued and this amount should be added to the invoice price.

A copy goes to the purchaser's Accounts Department, another is retained by the seller's Accounts Department and one may go to the Sales Department.

15.9   Statement

Traders do not generally pay each invoice as it arrives. A period of up to one month is usually allowed for payment. So a trader will receive a statement of his account with the supplier which lists all the invoices issued during the month, together with any outstanding previous balance. Credit/debit notes and payments received will also be listed, giving the current balance outstanding and due for settlement. A copy will be retained by the seller's Accounts Department.

Fig. 15.6   A statement

```
CARDINAL OFFICE SUPPLIES
55 High Street
OLD TOWN
Bucks
```

STATEMENT

To: Starlight Tours   Date: 31.1.88
      94 Victoria Street
      NEW TOWN
      Herts   AE1 3FG

Date	Reference	Debits	Credits	Balance
11.10.87	76198	£87.65		£87.65
18.10.87	76243	£34.75		£122.40
30.10.87	76320	£55.47		£177.87

Terms: 30 days net

15.10   Computerised Procedures

The sales and purchasing procedures and documents are now frequently handled by the company computer. When an order is received the details are recorded on the computer files. The program can add this information to the customer/supplier account, and to the company statistics held. All the documents can be produced by the computer, which will calculate VAT, discounts and totals. At the end of the month the statement can be produced from the records held and payment recorded when it is received.

Questions

1 Put the following documents in the correct order of production: quotation, statement, order, enquiry, invoice.
2 Name the types of discount which might be offered to traders and the circumstances of their use.
3 Which items of information would be most important on a quotation?
4 In what circumstances might it be necessary to issue a credit note?

Chapter 16

Methods of Payment

There are several methods by which business payments are made. The banks, Post Office and building societies offer a wide range of services to business and personal customers.

16.1 Bank Services

The major British banks offer a wide range of services to their customers. The main aspects of their services are:

— providing safe facilities for making payments;
— paying interest on deposits;
— lending money to approved clients;
— handling clients' payments by direct debit, standing order and credit transfer systems;
— providing methods of making payments abroad;
— discounting bills of exchange;
— providing credit cards and cash dispensing facilities;
— issuing travellers' cheques and foreign currency;
— handling clients' valuables, securities and investments;
— acting as trustees and executors;
— offering advisory services to businesses.

Bank accounts

The main types of accounts which they offer are:

Deposit
This is usually a savings account: a customer receives interest on the balance. Notice of withdrawal may be required, especially for large sums. No cheque book or cheque card is issued.

119

Budget
Approved customers calculate their total annual expenses on such items as gas, electricity, car maintenance, holidays, clothing, etc. A regular monthly transfer of 1/12 of this total sum is made to the budget account from the customer's current account. A separate cheque book is issued for the budget account and payments are made throughout the year regardless of the balance in hand. The account may be overdrawn at times, when interest is charged, and have a credit balance at other periods, but no interest is accrued. At the end of twelve months the expenses and in-payments should be equal.

Current
This is the most widely used account, and it is used to make and receive payments as necessary. Cheques are drawn for withdrawals and payments (Fig. 16.1), and paying-in slips (Fig. 16.2) are required with deposits. Interest is not received on a credit balance in a current account but charges are made when it is overdrawn.

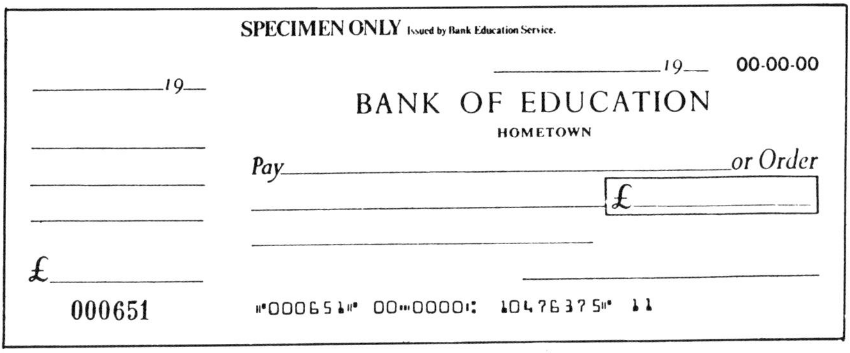
SPECIMEN ONLY Issued by Bank Education Service.
______ 19__ 00-00-00
______ 19__
BANK OF EDUCATION
HOMETOWN
Pay ______ or Order
£ ______
£ ______
000651
⑈000651⑈ 00⑆0000⑆ 10476375⑈ 11

Fig. 16.1 A cheque

Cheques

A cheque is a written order to the bank to pay the stated amount to the payee.

Open cheque
An open cheque is one without a 'crossing' and it may be cashed over a bank counter.

Specimen Only Issued by Banking Information Service

bank giro credit

Date _____

Code No.

To be used by customer for own account at other branches/Banks

Bank _____

Cashier's Stamp **To** Branch _____
(Block Capitals)

Account _____ Account No. _____

Paid in by _____

£50 notes	
£20 notes	
£10 notes	
£5 notes	
£1	
50p	
Silver	
Bronze	
Total Cash	
Postal Orders	
Cheques etc.
(Listed overleaf)	
Rem £	

POSTAL ORDERS   CHEQUES

FORWARD

Fig. 16.2   A paying-in slip

Crossed cheque

Most British cheques have two parallel lines printed across the face. This prevents a cheque being cashed across a counter as it must be paid into a bank, building society or Post Office account.

A special crossing restricts payment further. By writing between the crossing lines the specific account or branch can be named, e.g.

Fig. 16.3   A special crossing

Endorsement
The payee must sign the back of an 'or Order' cheque if he wishes
to pass it to another person instead of paying it into his bank.

Stale cheque
A cheque is valid for payment for six months, then it becomes stale
and the bank will refuse to accept it.

Post-dated cheque
A customer may write a date ahead of time on a cheque. The bank
will not accept the cheque for payment until that date.

Alterations
If an error is made, it may be corrected neatly and accepted by the
bank when the drawer's initials are signed beside the alteration.

Dishonoured
A bank may refuse to accept a cheque for payment:

— if words and figures are different;
— if the date is wrong or it is post-dated;
— if there is insufficient balance in the account to meet the sum;
— if the signature does not match their records;
— if an alteration is not initialled;
— if payment has been stopped by the drawer;
— due to the drawer's death, bankruptcy or insanity.

Stopping a cheque
Payment of a cheque can be stopped by the account holder before
it has been cleared through the banking system. Written
instructions are required by the bank. If the cheque is later
released for payment, further written instructions must be given.
This may be necessary if goods or services are at fault. However,
cheques supported by a cheque guarantee card cannot be stopped.

Cheque cards
Banks issue current account holders with a plastic card which
guarantees payment of cheques up to £50. Most traders require
this guarantee of payment. Customers can also cash cheques at
any bank or branch with the support of this card. A cheque cannot
be stopped if it carries the card number on the reverse and is within
the cash limit.

Eurocheques
All the major banks offer special cheques for customers to use

abroad. They can be written in many foreign currencies to pay for goods or services, or to withdraw cash from any bank displaying the Eurocheque sign. This is often a more convenient method of payment than using travellers' cheques.

Bill of exchange
This is a convenient method of payment when dealing with overseas customers. It is drawn up by the exporter stating the amount owed and the date the sum is due. It is signed by the importer, so making it a legally binding promise to pay. A bank will also arrange to sign the bill of exchange as a guarantee of payment. These bills are usually valid for three months. The exporter has the assurance of payment without the need to give credit to an unknown foreign customer.

Standing orders

A customer can instruct his bank to initiate payment of a fixed sum from his current account to a named business or person on specified dates. The instruction is given in writing and alterations and cancellation must also be in writing.

Direct debit

This system also requires written instructions to the account holder's bank to make payments from a current account. The payments may be fixed or variable amounts, at regular or irregular intervals. The payee requests the bank to pay from the customer's account. Written confirmation is not required for small changes in amount or frequency but cancellation must be confirmed in writing.

Credit transfer

When a customer has several creditors to pay, he can send a list to the bank giving names, account details and amounts, together with one total cheque. The bank arranges for the amounts to be transferred to the accounts listed, which may be at different banks and branches.

The customer saves time in preparing cheques or handling cash and dealing with accompanying papers, as well as postage costs.

The service can be used by businesses or personal customers. This is a popular method of paying salaries and wages as it is secure and saves much time.

Credit cards

A credit card enables a customer to pay for goods or services without writing a cheque and to withdraw cash from a cash dispensing machine. The customer has a personal number which is noted by the seller who makes a return to the card company. The card company sends out monthly accounts to the card holders. Each card holder has a credit limit and must pay at least 5% of the total debt each month. Interest is charged at a high rate on any balance unpaid. Barclaycard and Visa are the best known credit cards but some retail groups have their own schemes which are sometimes linked with regular monthly payments to a 'budget' account.

Charge cards

There are also plastic cards against which purchases may be charged, but when the monthly account is received the full amount is payable. These are useful for employees using company expense accounts for travel, entertaining, etc. Some retail groups run their own card systems also. American Express is a well-known charge card.

Cash dispensing machines

Plastic cards are also available from banks, building societies and the Post Office for use in the cash machines installed inside and/or outside most of their premises. Each machine is linked to a computer and will issue up to £100 per day, provided the customer's account has sufficient funds. Each customer has a personal number which must be memorised and used to operate the machine.

Statements

A computerised statement is sent to each bank account holder at regular intervals. This details the movement of funds in and out of the account, including standing orders, direct debits, etc. It gives a balance after each entry. The account holder should check the statement against his own records to ensure that it is correct and to see whether any charges have been imposed by the bank.

Fig. 16.4 A bank statement

Lloyds Bank

Statement of account with Lloyds Bank Plc

LANCASTER

STATEMENT

GRANT MR T E & MRS E P

Sheet number	
J	163	*

Description of entries

BGC Bank Giro Credit
C/P Cashpoint Withdrawal
DIV Dividend
D/D Direct Debit
S/O Standing Order

Cheques are designated
by the serial number

All entries to
26 JUL 86
inclusive are
complete.

Account number

0329867

Date	Particulars		Payments		Receipts		Balance *When overdrawn marked OD*		
1986	Opening Balance						1732	40	*
27JUN		343210	33	77			1698	63	*
28JUN	HERTS C C				830	57			
	PARK STREET LUTON	C/P 2	50	00			2479	20	*
1JLY		303211	19	89			2459	31	*
3JLY	BANK GIRO CREDIT				58	50			
		303212	1320	00			1197	81	*
4JLY		303213	37	94			1159	87	*
5JLY		303214	72	66					
	ANBS	S/O	129	34					
	PARK STREET LUTON	C/P 2	50	00					
	LEGAL AND GENERAL	D/D	23	36			884	51	*
9JLY		303215	5	27					
		303216	100	00			779	24	*
11JLY		303217	28	88			750	36	*

The items and balance shown should be verified. Details of rates and calculation of any interest charged are available on request to this branch.
The Bank is not liable for loss or delay caused directly or indirectly by industrial action or by circumstances beyond its control.

Reconciling the statement

Some recent payments may not appear on the bank statement, or items such as charges or interest may have been included which the account holder has not recorded. Therefore, when checking a statement it is necessary to list the items not yet cleared and the extra items to be deducted. The debit and credit figures can then be recalculated and the final balance should agree with the account holder's own records. If not, the discrepancy should be identified and queried with the bank.

16.2 Post Office Services

Cash

Coins and notes are usually only used to settle small sums in business and if posted the registered service must be used.

Postal orders

These orders are convenient for sending small sums through the post. Various values are available and a fee (poundage) is charged. The counterfoil should be retained for reference.

A postal order is valid for six months from the final day of the issuing month. For payment only through a bank, a postal order may be crossed in the same manner as a bank cheque. Generally the payee signs the postal order and cashes it across the post office counter.

International payments

British postal orders may be cashed in some countries but payment is more commonly made through the banking or Girobank systems.

Girobank

The Girobank is a wholly-owned subsidiary of the Post Office, providing a wide range of banking services and using the national network of post offices.

Fig. 16.5 A Giro transfer form

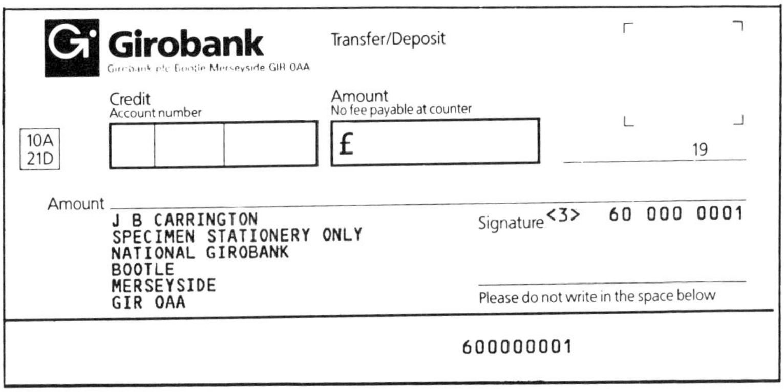

Girobank
Girobank plc Bootle Merseyside GIR 0AA
Transfer/Deposit

Credit
Account number

Amount
No fee payable at counter
£

10A
21D

19

Amount

J B CARRINGTON
SPECIMEN STATIONERY ONLY
NATIONAL GIROBANK
BOOTLE
MERSEYSIDE
GIR 0AA

Signature <3> 60 000 0001

Please do not write in the space below

600000001

Fig. 16.6 A Girobank cheque

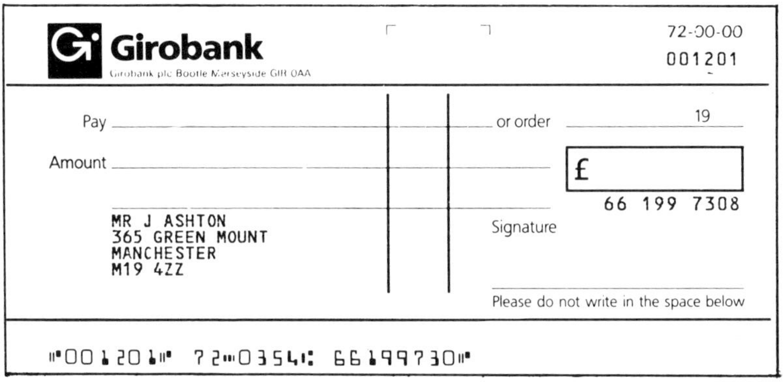
Girobank
Girobank plc Bootle Merseyside GIR 0AA
72-00-00
001201
Pay or order 19
Amount £
66 199 7308
MR J ASHTON
365 GREEN MOUNT
MANCHESTER
M19 4ZZ
Signature
Please do not write in the space below

Current account
There are no charges for personal customers whilst their account remains in credit. Charges are made for debit transactions while an account is overdrawn.

Cheque card
This is a plastic card which guarantees payments up to £50 and which may be used for drawing cash up to £100 at nominated post offices.

Cash withdrawals
Up to £50 may be withdrawn at any post office each working day (with a cheque card) or every other day at either of the two nominated offices without a cheque card.

Transfer of funds
There is a free service for making payments to other Girobank account holders.

Statement
A statement is received after each credit entry or ten debit entries listing details of the transactions and stating the running balance.

The Girobank also offers deposit accounts, personal loans, mortgages, credit/finance, foreign currency, etc. Visa credit cards, insurance services and automated banking 24 hours per day are available.

Additional services to business include:

— marshalling of funds into central accounts;
— direct debit, standing orders, credit transfer;

- — facilities for the deposit of company takings;
- — money market deposits;
- — investment services;
- — cash transfer through clearing houses;
- — international money transmission and travel finance;
- — credit facilities, i.e. loans, overdrafts;
- — arrangements with building societies for their customers to make deposits and withdrawals from their building society accounts at post offices.

Transcash

This is a service through which anyone can pay cash into a Giro account at any post office. A message may be included on the back of the special payment slip, which is sent to the account holder after the transaction has been completed. This service is widely used by large organisations such as mail order companies, and the electricity, gas and water boards, who provide their own payment slips. International payments can also be made.

Fig. 16.7 A Transcash form

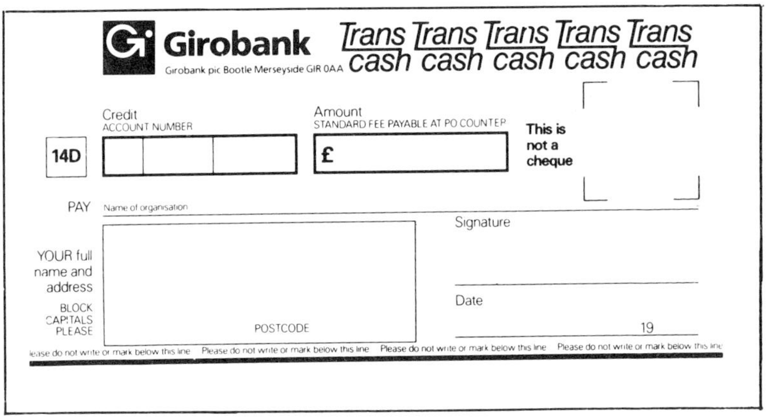
Girobank
Girobank plc Bootle Merseyside GIR 0AA
Trans cash Trans cash Trans cash Trans cash Trans cash
14D
Credit
ACCOUNT NUMBER
Amount
STANDARD FEE PAYABLE AT PO COUNTER
£
This is not a cheque
PAY Name of organisation
Signature
YOUR full name and address
BLOCK CAPITALS PLEASE
POSTCODE
Date
19
Please do not write or mark below this line Please do not write or mark below this line Please do not write or mark below this line Please do not write or mark below this line

There is a Freepay facility where the payee pays the counter fee. Cheques as well as cash are accepted for these payments.

16.3 Building Societies

Most building societies offer personal account services comparable with the bank and Girobank current and deposit accounts. However, the building societies are increasing their involvement in traditional banking services due to changes in the rules governing their trading. Legislation is steadily increasing the range of services which building societies are allowed to provide and these are in direct competition with the major banks.

16.4 Electronic Funds Transfer

This system handles the automatic flow of funds between customers using their own computer linked to that of their building society or bank. Customers have access to their own account and can check entries and balance.

To transfer funds instructions are relayed to the computer and the transaction is completed without cheque writing. The advantages to business include:

— greater control of finances and cash flow;
— faster transfer to gain interest;
— more effective planning;
— simpler preparation of reconciliation statements;
— a workstation to update company records.

The banks and building societies gain by:

— reduced costs;
— quicker cheque clearing and payment credits.

In addition to business use, this system is increasingly available to personal customers. They can transfer funds from one account to another to cover payments or gain interest. In the future Electronic Funds Transfer at Point of Sale (EFT-POS) will be used to settle retail payments immediately at shop cash desks. It will eliminate the need for cheques to be written. The debit will be made immediately by the computer.

Questions

1 Name three types of bank account. With which of these are you entitled to a cheque book?
2 Explain the following terms in relation to cheques: stopped; post-dated; crossed.
3 How does the credit transfer (Bank Giro) system work?
4 What is the value of a cheque guarantee card? What effect does it have if you wish to stop payment of a cheque?
5 Your employer is travelling abroad on business; name the methods by which he can pay any expenses incurred whilst he is away.

6   What is Electronic Funds Transfer? State the advantages this system offers for business customers.
7   What is the Transcash service and who might use it?
8   What are the services offered by the National Girobank to business customers?

Chapter 17

Accounts Department

The Accounts department is responsible for maintaining accurate records of the company's financial transactions and it generally includes a cashier's section. The work mainly involves dealing with customers' and suppliers' accounts, handling cash flow, petty cash, salaries and wages, statistics for management and end of year accounts. A costing section would also be responsible for calculating the unit cost of individual activities and completed products to ensure that they continue to trade at a profit.

17.1   Computerised Accounting

Most companies now use a computer to handle their accounting records. The increased speed of working ensures that information on the state of individual accounts and the company's financial situation is up-to-date. Quick action can be taken to follow up overdue accounts and make credit control checks on potential customers. The statistical data provided for management is available quickly and decisions on changes can be implemented more rapidly.

17.2   Accounting Terms

Simultaneous entry

Documents are designed so that details are recorded manually on several forms at the same time, i.e. payslip, employee record and payroll sheet. This avoids errors in copying from one document to another.

Double-entry

Each transaction is recorded twice, once on the debit and once on the credit side of the accounting records.

Journals (Day Books)—also called books of original entry

Transactions are recorded daily in date order. Books involved are Purchases and Sales Day Books, Purchases and Sales Returns Books, Cash Books and Petty Cash Books.

Trial balance

This procedure checks the accuracy of the records and organises the accounts before preparation of the end of year accounts. It can be undertaken by Accounts Department staff several times during the year.

Audit

An audit is a systematic check on accounting activities. An internal company audit is usually conducted to find and correct any errors. An external audit is carried out by an independent firm of accountants and is compulsory for limited companies under the Companies Act.

Credit control

It is necessary to keep a check on the amount of credit allowed to each customer. New customers should be assessed from references, including their bank, and existing customers from their payment record.

17.3   Petty Cash

Every business incurs a variety of small expenses and these are generally met from petty cash. The most popular method of handling this is by the Imprest System.

An amount is taken from the company Cash Book to start the petty cash period, usually a month or less. Each time an expense is incurred a petty cash voucher is completed and a receipt is attached.

Fig. 17.1   A petty cash voucher

Petty Cash Voucher	Folio			
	Date			

Required for	VAT amount		Amount including VAT	
	£	p	£	p
Postage Stamps *60 × 18p*		—	10	80
Total	—		10	80

Signature   *W. Field*

Authorised by   *R. Watson*

Each voucher is numbered (Folio No.), dated and gives brief details of the expense together with VAT amount. It should carry two signatures—one of the person spending the money and the other as authorisation to reimburse the amount.

A Petty Cash Book is kept showing the total amounts paid out and detailing the type of expense in separate analysis columns. The book should be 'balanced' regularly at the end of the petty cash period or when more money is needed. The accuracy of the records can be checked easily as the totals of the analysis columns must be equal to the total of the total column when the book is 'balanced'.

The petty cash system is then reimbursed by the amount paid out, bringing the float (imprest) back to the original amount.

The cash must be kept in a lockable box and stored in a secure place. One person only should be responsible for handling it. At any time the amount of cash in the box plus the value of the vouchers should equal the original imprest. Frequent random checks should be made for security.

Fig. 17.2   Example of a petty cash book page

PETTY CASH BOOK

Dr.   Cr.

Received	Date	Particulars	Voucher number	Total Paid Out	Post	Stationery etc.	Travel	Office Expenses	VAT
50 00	1/3/88	To Cash							
	1/3	Magazines	311	3 75				3 75	
	4/3	Stamps	312	10 80	10 80				
	7/3	Window Cleaning	313	11 50				10 00	1 50
	11/3	Folders	314	6 90		6 00			0 90
	16/3	W P Discs	315	13 80		12 00			1 80
		TOTAL		46 75	10 80	18 00	—	13 75	4 20
	16/3	By Balance c/d		3 25					
50 00				50 00					
3 25	16/3	To Balance b/d							
46 75	16/3	" Cash							

17.4 Salaries and Wages

Earnings

Employed persons receive payment for their work in the form of either a salary, which is quoted as an annual amount and usually paid monthly, or a wage, which is quoted as an hourly rate and usually paid weekly. Salaried staff are generally given time off in lieu of extra hours worked but wage-earners are paid for such overtime, often at premium (higher than basic) rates.

Gross earnings can also be increased in the following ways.

Bonus
This is an additional payment for increased output/turnover.

Increment
This is a fixed annual increase in salary not dependent on performance.

Merit award
This is an increase in salary based on the employee's performance of his/her duties.

Commission
This is a percentage of the value of business achieved by sales personnel.

Profit-sharing
This is a proportion of company profits paid to all employees at the year end, often a percentage of their annual salary/wage.

'Perks' (perquisites)
These are additional non-cash benefits provided for individuals or all employees, e.g. rent-free accommodation, non-contributory pension scheme, low-cost loans, company car, discounts on purchases, travel and expense allowances.

Statutory deductions

Before the earnings are received certain compulsory deductions are made.

Income Tax
Employees are assessed for tax on the PAYE (Pay As You Earn) system. Each person is allocated a Tax Code Number according to the allowances made to them by the Inland Revenue. Tables of figures are provided for companies to deduct the appropriate

Fig. 17.3 A P45 form

P45   **Details of EMPLOYEE LEAVING**   **PART 1**

		District number	Reference number
1.	PAYE reference		

2. National Insurance number

3. Surname
Use CAPITAL letters   Mr. Mrs. Miss

First two forenames
Use CAPITAL letters

SPECIMEN

4. Date of leaving *(in figures)*	Day	Month	Year 19

5. Code at date of leaving	Code	Week 1 or Month 1
If Week 1 or Month 1 basis applies, please also write "X" in the box marked "Week 1 or Month 1"		

6. Last entries on Deductions Working Sheet *If Week 1 or Month 1 basis applies, complete item 7 instead*		Week	Month
	Week or Month number		
	Total pay to date	£	p
	Total tax to date	£	p

7. Week 1 or Month 1 basis applies	Total pay in this employment	£	p
	Total tax in this employment	£	p

8. Works Number		9. Branch, Contract Department, etc.	

10. Employee's private address ....
....
.... Postcode ....

11. I certify that the details entered at items 1 to 9 above are correct.

Employer

Address   SPECIMEN

Date   Postcode

INSTRUCTIONS TO EMPLOYER

● Complete this form according to the "Employee leaving" instructions on the form P8. Make sure the details are clear on all three parts.

● Detach Part 1 and send it to your Tax Office **IMMEDIATELY.**

● Hand Parts 2 and 3 (unseparated) to your employee **WHEN HE LEAVES.**

● IF THE EMPLOYEE HAS DIED, please write "D" in this box and send ALL THREE PARTS of this form (unseparated) to your Tax Office **IMMEDIATELY.**

For Tax Office use

For Centre 1 use		
Amended	M/E	P

P45   HPB 1439 8/86

amounts from employees' earned income each week or month. The tax year runs from 6 April of one year to 5 April of the following year. Self-employed people are assessed for tax liability on a different system.

When a person leaves an employer he is given an P45 form (Fig. 17.3). This is a statement of the total earnings and tax paid for the year to date. The form is in three parts. One part is sent to the tax office by the employer and the individual gives the rest to his new employer.

National Insurance (NI)
Contributions are assessed as a percentage of gross earnings within minimum and maximum figures, and tables are again provided for accurate deductions to be made. The National Insurance system is designed to provide the money for unemployment and sickness payments, government pensions, maternity benefits, etc.

Voluntary deductions

Employees may also request further deductions to be made from their gross pay before they receive payment. These include:

SAYE (Save As You Earn)
This is a Post Office savings scheme whereby a minimum of £5 is deducted each month for five years. Interest accrues on the account.

Trade Union dues
Subscriptions may be deducted through an agreement between employers and unions.

Recreation/sports club
A small fee may be levied towards the provision of company leisure facilities.

Pension
A contributory company pension payment may be made.

Assessment

The net income of each hourly-paid employee is found by totalling the hours worked as recorded on a clock card (Fig. 17.5) or time sheet.

Multiply this figure by the hourly rate to find the gross pay.

Using Table A overleaf look up his tax code number to ascertain the amount to date that is not taxed.

Fig. 17.4   Extracts from Income Tax Tables A and B

WEEK 4
Apr 27 to May 3

TABLE A—FREE PAY

Code	Total free pay to date £	Code	Total free pay to date £	Code	Total free pay to date £	Code	Total free pay to date £	Code	Total free pay to date £	Code	Total free pay to date £	Code	Total free pay to date £	Code	Total free pay to date £
41	32·24	101	78·40	161	124·56	221	170·72	281	216·88	341	263·00	401	309·16	461	355·32
42	33·00	102	79·16	162	125·32	222	171·48	282	217·64	342	263·80	402	309·96	462	356·08
43	33·80	103	79·96	163	126·08	223	172·24	283	218·40	343	264·56	403	310·72	463	356·88
44	34·56	104	80·72	164	126·88	224	173·00	284	219·16	344	265·32	404	311·48	464	357·64
45	35·32	105	81·48	165	127·64	225	173·80	285	219·96	345	266·08	405	312·24	465	358·40
46	36·08	106	82·24	166	128·40	226	174·56	286	220·72	346	266·88	406	313·00	466	359·16
47	36·88	107	83·00	167	129·16	227	175·32	287	221·48	347	267·64	407	313·80	467	359·96
48	37·64	108	83·80	168	129·96	228	176·08	288	222·24	348	268·40	408	314·56	468	360·72
49	38·40	109	84·56	169	130·72	229	176·88	289	223·00	349	269·16	409	315·32	469	361·48
50	39·16	110	85·32	170	131·48	230	177·64	290	223·80	350	269·96	410	316·08	470	362·24
51	39·96	111	86·08	171	132·24	231	178·40	291	224·56	351	270·72	411	316·88	471	363·00
52	40·72	112	86·88	172	133·00	232	179·16	292	225·32	352	271·48	412	317·64	472	363·80
53	41·48	113	87·64	173	133·80	233	179·96	293	226·08	353	272·24	413	318·40	473	364·56
54	42·24	114	88·40	174	134·56	234	180·72	294	226·88	354	273·00	414	319·16	474	365·32
55	43·00	115	89·16	175	135·32	235	181·48	295	227·64	355	273·80	415	319·96	475	366·08
56	43·80	116	89·96	176	136·08	236	182·24	296	228·40	356	274·56	416	320·72	476	366·88
57	44·56	117	90·72	177	136·88	237	183·00	297	229·16	357	275·32	417	321·48	477	367·64
58	45·32	118	91·48	178	137·64	238	183·80	298	229·96	358	276·08	418	322·24	478	368·40
59	46·08	119	92·24	179	138·40	239	184·56	299	230·72	359	276·88	419	323·00	479	369·16
60	46·88	120	93·00	180	139·16	240	185·32	300	231·48	360	277·64	420	323·80	480	369·96

see page 2

6

TABLE B

TAX DUE ON TAXABLE PAY FROM £1 TO £360

Total TAXABLE PAY to date £	Total TAX DUE to date £	Total TAXABLE PAY to date £	Total TAX DUE to date £	Total TAXABLE PAY to date £	Total TAX DUE to date £	Total TAXABLE PAY to date £	Total TAX DUE to date £	Total TAXABLE PAY to date £	Total TAX DUE to date £	Total TAXABLE PAY to date £	Total TAX DUE to date £
1	0.27	61	16.47	121	32.67	181	48.87	241	65.07	301	81.27
2	0.54	62	16.74	122	32.94	182	49.14	242	65.34	302	81.54
3	0.81	63	17.01	123	33.21	183	49.41	243	65.61	303	81.81
4	1.08	64	17.28	124	33.48	184	49.68	244	65.88	304	82.08
5	1.35	65	17.55	125	33.75	185	49.95	245	66.15	305	82.35
6	1.62	66	17.82	126	34.02	186	50.22	246	66.42	306	82.62
7	1.89	67	18.09	127	34.29	187	50.49	247	66.69	307	82.89
8	2.16	68	18.36	128	34.56	188	50.76	248	66.96	308	83.16
9	2.43	69	18.63	129	34.83	189	51.03	249	67.23	309	83.43
10	2.70	70	18.90	130	35.10	190	51.30	250	67.50	310	83.70
11	2.97	71	19.17	131	35.37	191	51.57	251	67.77	311	83.97
12	3.24	72	19.44	132	35.64	192	51.84	252	68.04	312	84.24
13	3.51	73	19.71	133	35.91	193	52.11	253	68.31	313	84.51
14	3.78	74	19.98	134	36.18	194	52.38	254	68.58	314	84.78
15	4.05	75	20.25	135	36.45	195	52.65	255	68.85	315	85.05
16	4.32	76	20.52	136	36.72	196	52.92	256	69.12	316	85.32
17	4.59	77	20.79	137	36.99	197	53.19	257	69.39	317	85.59
18	4.86	78	21.06	138	37.26	198	53.46	258	69.66	318	85.86

Deduct this from the gross pay to date figure on his record to find the taxable income.

This figure is found in Table B, which states the amount of tax payable to date.

Deduct from this the amount of tax paid up to the previous week and the difference is the tax to be deducted for the current week.

Look up on the NI tables to find the contribution due.

Note any voluntary deductions.

Total the various deductions and take this figure from the gross pay figure to ascertain the net pay to be received.

The same procedure is followed for salaried staff based on the appropriate proportion of their annual salary, i.e. one calendar month's pay equals one-twelfth annual salary.

Fig. 17.5   A clock card

NAME T Scott NO 6147				
DEPARTMENT Trim Shop				
WEEK ENDING 30.4.88 | WEEK NO 4				
DAY	IN	OUT	IN	OUT	TOTAL HOURS
MON	0758	1200	1300	1701	
TUES	0757	1201	1300	1930	
WED	0759	1201	1259	1930	
THUR	0758	1200	1301	2000	
FRI	0758	1201	1301	1700	
SAT	0859	1200			
SUN	0900	1200			
TOTAL					

FOR OFFICE USE ONLY

Ordinary time____hours @ £
Overtime   ____hours @ £
        ____hours @ £
        ____hours @ £

At the end of every tax year a P60 form is issued to each employee. This is a statement of the gross and net pay figures for the year, with Income Tax and National Insurance contributions paid.

17.5   Cash Analysis

When a sum of money is required with specific quantities of coins and notes, e.g. for wages paid in cash, it is necessary to calculate

Fig. 17.6   A pay slip

			£	p
Name T Scott				
Week/Month 4	Date 30/4	Tax Code No 349		
EARNINGS	Basic		120	00
	Overtime		61	50
	Bonus			
	Commission			
	GROSS PAY		181	50
DEDUCTIONS	Gross Pay to Date		576	16
	Tax Free Pay		269	16
	Taxable Pay to date		307	00
	Tax due to date		82	89
	Tax Paid to date		60	72
	Tax Refund			
	TAX PAYABLE		22	17
	N I Contribution		16	34
	1. SAYE		6	00
	2. Social Club		1	00
	3. Union Sub		2	50
	4.			
	TOTAL DEDUCTIONS		48	01
	NET PAY		133	49
	Expenses etc			
	TOTAL AMOUNT PAYABLE		133	49

the exact breakdown of notes and coins needed. The bank is informed of the total amount and the quantity of each denomination required. For example, the employees in the Trim Shop for Week 4, may have net pay as follows:

T Scott	£133.49
R Johnson	£145.62
T Pickett	£127.55
M Marshall	£108.33
Total	£514.99

Cash Analysis:			
	£20 notes	24 =	480.00
	£10 notes	1 =	10.00
	£5 notes	3 =	15.00
	£1 coins	8 =	8.00
	50p coins	2 =	1.00
	20p coins	3 =	0.60
	10p coins	2 =	0.20
	5p coins	2 =	0.10
	2p coins	4 =	0.08
	1p coins	1 =	0.01
		Total	£514.99

17.6   Computerised Payroll

There are now many computer applications to assist payroll handling. The tax and NI tables are held in the store together with the latest employees' payment records. When new figures are keyed in the process is rapidly completed and the payroll records are updated automatically. The individual payslips and company records are also printed. A company's payroll can be processed quickly by computer, so leaving payroll staff more time for other work. Cash analysis is also rapidly calculated by the computer.

Questions

1   What is an audit? Why is it advisable to undertake this activity internally?
2   What is a petty cash imprest?
3   Why does a petty cash voucher carry two signatures?
4   List the methods by which a person's basic salary or wage might be increased.
5   What type of deduction from pay is SAYE? What do the letters represent?
6   What is a P45 and what information does it give?
7   When does an employee receive a P60?

Index

abbreviated dialling   30
account call   34
accounting terms   131
ADC   33
addendum   66
addressing machines   16
ad hoc   66
adjournment   66
Admail   19
advice/delivery notes   115
agenda   61, 66
AGM   66
Airstream   24
All-Up postal service   24
alphabetical filing   76
alpha-numerical filing   76
alterations to cheques   122
amendment   66
annual general meetings   60
answering calls   30
Articles of Association   2, 66
audit   132
automatic redialling   30

bank accounts   119
bank dictating system   84
bank services   119
bar charts   52
bill of exchange   123
board meetings   60
bonus   135
books of original entry   132
break-even charts   55
briefing meetings   61
budget account   120
building societies   128
bulk rebate postal service   26
bulletins   46
Bureaufax   38
Business Reply Service   18

call back   29
call barring   30
call-connect   29
call diversion   29
call logging   29
call transfer   30
card drawers   73
card holders   73
cash analysis   139
cash dispensing machines   124
cash on delivery postal service   26
casting vote   66

cellphones   32
cellular offices   9
central government departments   3
centralised records   70
centralised services   7
centring, on typewriters   83
chairman, duties at a meeting   65
charge cards   124
cheque cards   122
cheques   120
chronological filing   77
circular letters   45
classification of records   76
colour coded filing   78
colour transfer   97
commission   135
communication services, books
   on   101
Compensation Fee parcels   23
composition of letters   44
computerised accounting   131
computerised mail room
   equipment   16
computerised payroll   141
computerised sales/purchasing
   procedures   117
computerised stock control   109
computer records   79
computers   88
conference call   30
Confravision   36
consultation meetings   61
co-operatives   3
co-opted   67
co-ordinated meetings   61
cordless phones   32
credit call   34
credit control   132
credit cards   124
credit/debit notes   116
credit transfer   123
crossed cheque   121
cross referenced filing   78
current account   120

daisy wheel printers   92
databases   103
Datel   37
Datapost   20
Data Protection Act 1984   79
date stamping   11
day books   132
dealing with the Press   42

decentralised records   70
decimal filing   77
deductions from pay   135
departmental responsibilities   5
deposit account   119
dictating machines   84
direct debit   123
direct link dictating system   84
direct mail   26
discounts, sales/purchasing   112
discount postal services   26
dishonoured cheques   122
dot matrix printers   92
double-entry   132
dual spectrum copier   97
duplicators   96
duties of chairman   65
duties of secretary   65
dyeline (diazo) copier   95

earnings   135
edge punched cards   76
electronic filing cabinets   73
electronic funds transfer   129
electronic mail   37
electronic scanner   99
Electronic Yellow Pages   103
electrostatic copiers   94
endorsement of cheques   122
English language books   100
Eurocheques   122
executive meetings   61
ex officio   67
Express Delivery service   20
Express Overseas service   24
extended keyboard typewriters   82
extension group hunting   30
extraordinary general meetings   60
EYP   103

facsimile (fax)   87
filing equipment   71
filing guides   77
final digit filing   77
first class post   18
fixed time calls   33
flow charts   58
folding machine   17
follow up systems   78
franchise   4
franking machine   14, 15
Freefone   34
Freepost   19

Gantt charts   55
general reference books   102
Girobank   126
goods received note   115
government reference material   102

heat copier   97
holding companies   2
honorary   67
hotels and restaurants, books on   101
house journals   46
house style   44

Imtran   38
in attendance   67
income tax   135
incoming mail procedure   10
increment   135
information services, telephone   34
ink duplicators   96
ink jet printers   92
inserting and sealing machine   17
Intelpost   25
interchangeable heads   83
International Business Reply
   service   25
International Datapost   25
international payments   126
international reply coupons   25
International Telemessages   36
intra vires   67
inventories   108
invitations and replies   48
invoices   115

joint stock companies   2
journals   132
justification   83

laser printers   92
late posting facility   27
lateral filing   72
letter of enquiry   111
letter opener   11
letters, composition of   44
lie on the table   67
limited companies   2
line graphs   51
Linkline   35
local government   3

magnetic board   59
maintenance of equipment   83
making a call   31
maximum stock level   107
meeting, types of   60
memorandum, writing a   45
Memorandum of Association   2
merit award   135
microfilm   80
microwriter   86
minimum stock level   106
minutes   63
motion   67

National Insurance   137

nem con   67
networks and configurations   89
newsletters   46
notice of meeting   61
notices, display of   46
numerical filing   76

office design   9
office environment   7
office supplies   107
offset litho printer   98
open cheque   120
open plan   8
optimum order size   107
order   114
out cards   78
outgoing mail   12, 13
out of order   68

P45   136, 137
PABX   29
Packet Switchstream   35
parcel post   23
partnership   1
peg board   59
perks   135
personal calls   33
personal qualities, of receptionist   42
petty cash   132
phonecards   34
pictograms   53
pie charts   56, 57
pin board   59
plan chest/cabinet   73
PMBX   29
point of order   68
Postage Forward Parcels   23
postal orders   126
postal services   18
post-dated cheque   122
Post Office Guide   27
Post Office (payment) services   126
postponement   68
post restante   26
presenting a report   47
prepayment of post   26
Press, dealing with   42
Prestel   102
print size, of typewriters   83
printers   92
private box   26
private enterprise   1
profit-sharing   135
proxy   68
public corporations   3
public enterprise   2

quorum   68
quotation   113

radiopaging   33
radiophones   32
railway letter   20
reception area   43
reception duties   40
reconciling a bank statement   125
Recorded Delivery   21
redirection of mail   27
Red Star/Night Star   27
reference books   100
Registered Post   21
remittance book   11
repeat key   83
reports   47
requisition   111
resolution   68
responsibilities of:
    Board of Directors   6
    Chairman of meeting   65
    Company Secretary   7
    Secretary of meeting   65
rider   68
Rider services   23
Royal Mail Inland services   18
Royal Mail International services   24
Royal Mail letters and packets   18
Royal Mail parcels   23
rotary card holder   74
rotary filing   72
routing/circulation slip   12
running balance of stock   107

salaries and wages   135
SAYE   137
scales, postal   14
sealing machine   17
second class post   18
sector charts   53
secretary, duties at a meeting   65
security   42
Selectapost   26
ships' radiotelephones   32
simultaneous entry   131
sine die   68
skyphones   32
slot index   75
sole trader   1
Special Delivery   19
special search postal service   27
spirit duplicators   96
stale cheque   122
standard form letters   45
standing order, bank   123
standing orders   69
statement of account   116
statements, bank   124
statutory deductions from pay   135
stock record cards   105
stock records   105

stock, types of   105
stopping a cheque   122
strip index   75
summaries   47
Swiftair   25
switchboards   29
System X   30

tandem system   84
Telecom Gold   37
telecommunication services   35
telegrams   36
Telemessages   36, 47
telephone answering machines   31
telephones   29
telephone services   33–35
Teletex   37
teletext   38, 103
telex   35
telex messages   46
terms related to meetings   65–69
trade and industry, books on   101
Trakback   24
Transcash   128
travel, books on   101
trial balance   132
typewriters   82

ultra vires   69
unanimous   69
upgrading of equipment   83

valuation of stock   109
value added tax   116
vertical filing   71
Videostream   37
videotex   38, 102
viewdata   38, 102
visible edge cards   74
visitors, reception of   40
visual planning/control boards   58
voluntary deductions from pay   137

wheel card holder   74
white board   58
word processors   85
wrap-around   83

year books   102
year planner   59
Yellow Pages, Electronic (EYP)   103

Z charts   53

Chambers Commerce Series

The up-to-date series for school and college students, embracing the full range of business and vocational subjects.

Business Studies
Mark Juby

A comprehensive introduction to all aspects of business activity. The book covers the GCSE National Criteria in Business Studies, plus key areas of GCSE Commerce and Understanding Industrial Society courses. *Business Studies* is also geared to BTEC, LCCI, O/Standard Grade, RSA and SCOTVEC Courses.

Bookkeeping and Accounting
Harold Randall and David Beckwith

A comprehensive introduction, showing how financial records are made, maintained and used in business. The book is of especial value to students on AAT, BTEC, GCSE, LCCI, PEI, RSA and SCOTVEC syllabuses.

Typing
June Rowley

An introduction to basic typing theory and practice, ideal for a wide variety of secretarial and vocational courses including BTEC, CPVE, GCSE, LCCI, PEI, RSA and SCOTVEC.

Word Processing
Barbara Shaw

Covers everything from text editing to repagination and mail merge – all the practical word processing skills. Ideal for BTEC, LCCI, PEI, RSA and SCOTVEC courses.

Business Calculations
David Browning

A step-by-step guide to mathematics in business practice, from simple arithmetic to elementary statistics. Geared to courses of many varieties – CPVE, BTEC, LCCI, RSA and SCOTVEC; GCSE and O/Standard Grade Mathematics, professional training.

Business Law
Janice Elliot Montague

A practical introduction to the law, how it works and influences business procedures. *Business Law* covers relevant components of a host of syllabuses – ATT, ALS, BTEC, ICA, ICAS, ICMA, ILE, IOB, IPS, LCCI, SCCA, SCOTVEC.

The Business of Government
J. Denis Derbyshire

A straightforward introduction to British government, how it works in practice and how it influences business procedures. Covers key elements of Politics and Public Administration syllabuses, including BTEC, GCSE, RSA, O/Standard Grade, Modern Studies, SCOTVEC; an ideal reference text for A Level and Higher Grade courses.

Keyboarding
Derek Stananought

A book of exercises and advice on the skills needed in the age of new technology and the electronic office. Includes training material in basic keyboarding, proofreading, speed development, practical application of typing techniques. Ideal for secretarial and vocational courses – BTEC, CPVE, LCCI, PEI, RSA, SCOTVEC.

Secretarial Duties
Penny Anson

A complete guide to all the practical aspects of a professional secretary's work. Covers the syllabuses of the important courses, including BTEC, CPVE, LCCI, PEI, RSA, SCOTVEC.

Office Procedures
Ruth Martindale

A straightforward explanation of the work involved in running a modern office. Well illustrated, up-to-date, takes full account of the latest technology and procedures. Covers the syllabus requirements of BTEC, LCCI, Pitman, RSA, SCOTVEC.

Chambers Commercial Reference Series

Straightforward guides to all the essential terms used in the business world. Ideal for students on a wide range of introductory business and vocational courses. Written in clear, simple English.

Bookkeeping and Accounting Terms
Anthony Nielsen

Business Terms
John Simpson

Office Practice Terms
Josephine Hewitt

Office Technology Terms
Elizabeth King

Computer Terms
Sandra Carter

Business Law Terms
Stephen Foster

Printing and Publishing Terms
Martin H. Manser

Chambers
Office
Oracle

The ideal office reference book for
managers and secretaries everywhere.
The *Oracle* gives expert and helpful
advice on all aspects of office work –
composing letters, conducting
meetings, organising conferences,
choosing equipment, planning travel;
postal services, telecommunications,
banking, advertising are covered;
there are glossaries of business,
computing, medical, legal and
financial terms *plus a full*
English dictionary.